Rebuilding the Natural Environment, Grade 10

What if you could challenge your tenth graders to think about how innovation can make the world a better place for humans, while finding ways to sustain progress and conserve resources? With this volume in the *STEM Road Map Curriculum Series*, you can!

Rebuilding the Natural Environment outlines a journey that will steer your students toward authentic problem solving while grounding them in integrated STEM disciplines. Like the other volumes in the series, this book is designed to meet the growing need to infuse real-world learning into K–12 classrooms.

This interdisciplinary, four-lesson module uses project- and problem-based learning to help students connect their existing knowledge about energy production and its effects on the natural environment to create innovations in renewable sources of energy based on research evidence. Working in teams, students will design an innovative way to meet society's energy needs and develop a pitch to market their innovation, focusing on how the innovation will optimize human experiences while being mindful of the natural environment. To support this goal, students will do the following:

- Understand several forms of renewable, sustainable energy sources.

- Apply their understanding of how alternators are used to generate electricity in lab experiments, as well as explain how tools such as windmills and dams are used to operate them.

- Describe how electricity is generated in photovoltaic cells.

- Calculate the amount of electricity consumed by several household items and consider this consumption when determining the average monthly energy consumption of households around the world in comparison to U.S. households.

- Understand how fossil fuels have been used in the production of electricity and the impact they have had on the world's economy, humans' quality of life, and the earth.

- Identify several hindrances to the creation of new energy sources as well as ideas to counter them.

- List several factors that can be used to motivate people from all walks of life to use renewable and sustainable energies.

- Create a fictional company that uses renewable energies.

The *STEM Road Map Curriculum Series* is anchored in the Next Generation Science Standards, the Common Core State Standards, and the Framework for 21st Century Learning. In-depth and flexible, *Rebuilding the Natural Environment* can be used as a whole unit or in part to meet the needs of districts, schools, and teachers who are charting a course toward an integrated STEM approach.

Carla C. Johnson is Professor of Science Education in the College of Education and Office of Research and Innovation, and a Faculty Research Fellow at North Carolina State University in North Carolina, USA

Janet B. Walton is Senior Research Scholar at North Carolina State University in North Carolina, USA

Erin E. Peters-Burton is the Donna R. and David E. Sterling Endowed Professor in Science Education at George Mason University in Virginia, USA

T0383800

STEM ROAD MAP CURRICULUM SERIES

Series editors: Carla C. Johnson, Janet B. Walton, and Erin E. Peters-Burton

Map out a journey that will steer your students toward authentic problem solving as you ground them in integrated STEM disciplines.

Co-published by Routledge and NSTA Press, in partnership with the National Science Teaching Association, this K–12 curriculum series is anchored in the Next Generation Science Standards, the Common Core State Standards, and the Framework for 21st Century Learning. It was developed to meet the growing need to infuse real-world STEM learning into classrooms.

Each book is an in-depth module that uses project- and problem-based learning. First, your students are presented with a challenge. Then, they apply what they learn using science, social studies, English language arts, and mathematics. Engaging and flexible, each volume can be used as a whole unit or in part to meet the needs of districts, schools, and teachers who are charting a course toward an integrated STEM approach.

Modules are available from NSTA Press and Routledge, and organized under the following themes. For an update listing of the volumes in the series, please visit https://www.routledge.com/STEM-Road-Map-Curriculum-Series/book-series/SRM (for titles co-published by Routledge and NSTA Press), or www.nsta.org/book-series/stem-road-map-curriculum (for titles published by NSTA Press).

Co-published by Routledge and NSTA Press:

Optimizing the Human Experience:

- *Our Changing Environment, Grade K: STEM Road Map for Elementary School*
- *Genetically Modified Organisms, Grade 7: STEM Road Map for Middle School*
- *Rebuilding the Natural Environment, Grade 10: STEM Road Map for High School*
- *Mineral Resources, Grade 11: STEM Road Map for High School*

Cause and Effect:

- *Formation of the Earth, Grade 9: STEM Road Map for High School*

Published by NSTA Press:

Innovation and Progress:

- *Amusement Park of the Future, Grade 6: STEM Road Map for Elementary School*
- *Transportation in the Future, Grade 3: STEM Road Map for Elementary School*
- *Harnessing Solar Energy, Grade 4: STEM Road Map for Elementary School*
- *Wind Energy, Grade 5: STEM Road Map for Elementary School*
- *Construction Materials, Grade 11: STEM Road Map for High School*

The Represented World:

- *Patterns and the Plant World, Grade 1: STEM Road Map for Elementary School*
- *Investigating Environmental Changes, Grade 2: STEM Road Map for Elementary School*

- *Swing Set Makeover, Grade 3: STEM Road Map for Elementary School*
- *Rainwater Analysis, Grade 5: STEM Road Map for Elementary School*
- *Packaging Design, Grade 6: STEM Road Map for Middle School*
- *Improving Bridge Design, Grade 8: STEM Road Map for Middle School*
- *Radioactivity, Grade 11: STEM Road Map for High School*
- *Car Crashes, Grade 12: STEM Road Map for High School*

Cause and Effect:

- *Physics in Motion, Grade K: STEM Road Map for Elementary School*
- *Influence of Waves, Grade 1: STEM Road Map for Elementary School*
- *Natural Hazards, Grade 2: STEM Road Map for Elementary School*
- *Human Impacts on Our Climate, Grade 6: STEM Road Map for Middle School*
- *The Changing Earth, Grade 8: STEM Road Map for Middle School*
- *Healthy Living, Grade 10: STEM Road Map for High School*

Rebuilding the Natural Environment

Grade
10

STEM Road Map
for High School

Edited by Carla C. Johnson, Janet B. Walton, and
Erin E. Peters-Burton

NEW YORK AND LONDON

Cover images: icon © Shutterstock, map © Getty Images
Art and design for cover and interior adapted from NSTA Press

First published 2022
by Routledge
605 Third Avenue, New York, NY 10158

and by Routledge
4 Park Square, Milton Park, Abingdon, Oxon, OX14 4RN

Routledge is an imprint of the Taylor & Francis Group, an informa business

A co-publication with NSTA Press.

Library of Congress Cataloging-in-Publication Data
Names: Johnson, Carla C., 1969– editor. | Walton, Janet B., 1968– editor. | Peters-Burton, Erin E., editor.
Title: Rebuilding the natural environment, grade 10 / edited by Carla C. Johnson, Janet B. Walton, and Erin Peters-Burton.
Description: New York, NY : Routledge, 2022. | Series: STEM road map curriculum series | Includes bibliographical references and index.
Identifiers: LCCN 2021053113 | ISBN 9781032199771 (hbk) | ISBN 9781032199764 (pbk) | ISBN 9781003261711 (ebk)
Subjects: LCSH: Renewable energy sources—Study and teaching (Secondary) | Electric power production—Technological innovations—Study and teaching (Secondary) | Tenth grade (Education)
Classification: LCC TJ808 .R383 2022 | DDC 333.79/4—dc23/eng/20211116
LC record available at https://lccn.loc.gov/2021053113

ISBN: 978-1-032-19977-1 (hbk)
ISBN: 978-1-032-19976-4 (pbk)
ISBN: 978-1-003-26171-1 (ebk)

DOI: 10.4324/9781003261711

Typeset in Palatino LT Std
by Apex CoVantage, LLC

CONTENTS

Part 1: The STEM Road Map: Background, Theory, and Practice

Part 2: Rebuilding the Natural Environment: STEM Road Map Module

CONTENTS

4 Rebuilding the Natural Environment Lesson Plans **45**

Bradley Rankin, Anthony Pellegrino, Erin E. Peters-Burton,
Jennifer Drake Patrick, Janet B. Walton, and Carla C. Johnson

**5 Transforming Learning with Rebuilding the Natural Environment
and the *STEM Road Map Curriculum Series*** **117**

Carla C. Johnson

ABOUT THE EDITORS AND AUTHORS

Dr. Carla C. Johnson is a Professor of Science Education and ORI Faculty Research Fellow at NC State University in Raleigh, North Carolina. Dr. Johnson served (2015–2021) as the director of research and evaluation for the Department of Defense–funded Army Educational Outreach Program (AEOP), a global portfolio of STEM education programs, competitions, and apprenticeships. She has been a leader in STEM education for the past decade, serving as the director of STEM Centers, editor of the *School Science and Mathematics* journal, and lead researcher for the evaluation of Tennessee's Race to the Top–funded STEM portfolio. Dr. Johnson has published over 200 articles, books, book chapters, and curriculum books focused on STEM education. She is a former science and social studies teacher and was the recipient of the 2013 Outstanding Science Teacher Educator of the Year award from the Association for Science Teacher Education (ASTE), the 2012 Award for Excellence in Integrating Science and Mathematics from the School Science and Mathematics Association (SSMA), the 2014 award for best paper on Implications of Research for Educational Practice from ASTE, and the 2006 Outstanding Early Career Scholar Award from SSMA. Her research focuses on STEM education policy implementation, effective science teaching, and integrated STEM approaches.

Dr. Janet B. Walton is a Senior Research Scholar at NC State's College of Education in Raleigh, North Carolina. Formerly the STEM workforce program manager for Virginia's Region 2000 and founding director of the Future Focus Foundation, a nonprofit organization dedicated to enhancing the quality of STEM education in the region, she merges her economic development and education backgrounds to develop K–12 curricular materials that integrate real-life issues with sound cross-curricular content. Her research focus includes collaboration between schools and community stakeholders for STEM education, problem- and project-based learning pedagogies, online learning, and mixed methods research methodologies. She leverages this background to bring contextual STEM experiences into the classroom and provide students and educators with innovative resources and curricular materials. She is the former assistant director of evaluation of research and evaluation for the Department of Defense-funded Army Educational Outreach Program (AEOP), a global portfolio of STEM education programs, competitions, and apprenticeships and specializes in evaluation of STEM programs.

Dr. Erin E. Peters-Burton is the Donna R. and David E. Sterling Endowed Professor in Science Education at George Mason University in Fairfax, Virginia. She uses her experiences from 15 years as an engineer and secondary science, engineering, and mathematics teacher to develop research projects that directly inform classroom practice in science and engineering. Her research agenda is based on the idea that all students should build self-awareness of how they learn science and engineering. She works to help students see themselves as "science-minded" and help teachers create classrooms that support student skills to develop scientific knowledge. To accomplish this, she pursues research projects that investigate ways that students and teachers can use self-regulated learning theory in science and engineering, as well as how inclusive STEM schools can help students succeed. During her tenure as a secondary teacher, she had a National Board Certification in Early Adolescent Science and was an Albert Einstein Distinguished Educator Fellow for NASA. As a researcher, Dr. Peters-Burton has published over 100 articles, books, book chapters, and curriculum books focused on STEM education and educational psychology. She received the Outstanding Science Teacher Educator of the Year award from ASTE in 2016 and a Teacher of Distinction Award and a Scholarly Achievement Award from George Mason University in 2012, and in 2010 she was named University Science Educator of the Year by the Virginia Association of Science Teachers.

Dr. Tamara J. Moore is an associate professor of engineering education in the College of Engineering at Purdue University. Dr. Moore's research focuses on defining STEM integration through the use of engineering as the connection and investigating its power for student learning.

Dr. Toni A. May is an associate professor of assessment, research, and statistics in the School of Education at Drexel University in Philadelphia. Dr. May's research concentrates on assessment and evaluation in education, with a focus on K–12 STEM.

Jennifer Drake Patrick is an assistant professor of literacy education in the College of Education and Human Development at George Mason University. A former English language arts teacher, she focuses her research on disciplinary literacy.

Anthony Pellegrino is an assistant professor of social science in the College of Education at The University of Tennessee, Knoxville. He is a former social studies and history teacher whose research interests include youth-centered pedagogies and social science teacher preparation.

Bradley Rankin is a high school mathematics teacher at Wakefield High School in Arlington, Virginia. He has been teaching mathematics for 20 years, is board certified, and has a PhD in mathematics education leadership from George Mason University.

ACKNOWLEDGMENTS

This module was developed as a part of the STEM Road Map project (Carla C. Johnson, principal investigator). The Purdue University College of Education, General Motors, and other sources provided funding for this project.

See *www.routledge.com/9781138804234* for more information about *STEM Road Map: A Framework for Integrated STEM Education*.

PART 1

THE STEM ROAD MAP

BACKGROUND, THEORY, AND PRACTICE

OVERVIEW OF THE
STEM ROAD MAP CURRICULUM SERIES

Carla C. Johnson, Erin E. Peters-Burton, and Tamara J. Moore

The *STEM Road Map Curriculum Series* was conceptualized and developed by a team of STEM educators from across the United States in response to a growing need to infuse real-world learning contexts, delivered through authentic problem-solving pedagogy, into K–12 classrooms. The curriculum series is grounded in integrated STEM, which focuses on the integration of the STEM disciplines – science, technology, engineering, and mathematics – delivered across content areas, incorporating the Framework for 21st Century Learning along with grade-level-appropriate academic standards. The curriculum series begins in kindergarten, with a five-week instructional sequence that introduces students to the STEM themes and gives them grade-level-appropriate topics and real-world challenges or problems to solve. The series uses project-based and problem-based learning, presenting students with the problem or challenge during the first lesson, and then teaching them science, social studies, English language arts, mathematics, and other content, as they apply what they learn to the challenge or problem at hand.

Authentic assessment and differentiation are embedded throughout the modules. Each *STEM Road Map Curriculum Series* module has a lead discipline, which may be science, social studies, English language arts, or mathematics. All disciplines are integrated into each module, along with ties to engineering. Another key component is the use of STEM Research Notebooks to allow students to track their own learning progress. The modules are designed with a scaffolded approach, with increasingly complex concepts and skills introduced as students' progress through grade levels.

The developers of this work view the curriculum as a resource that is intended to be used either as a whole or in part to meet the needs of districts, schools, and teachers who are implementing an integrated STEM approach. A variety of implementation formats are possible, from using one standalone module at a given grade level to using all five modules to provide 25 weeks of instruction. Also, within each grade

DOI: 10.4324/9781003261711-2

band (K– 2, 3–5, 6–8, 9–12), the modules can be sequenced in various ways to suit specific needs.

STANDARDS-BASED APPROACH

The *STEM Road Map Curriculum Series* is anchored in the *Next Generation Science Standards (NGSS)*, the *Common Core State Standards for Mathematics (CCSS Mathematics)*, the *Common Core State Standards for English Language Arts (CCSS ELA)*, and the Framework for 21st Century Learning. Each module includes a detailed curriculum map that incorporates the associated standards from the particular area correlated to lesson plans. The STEM Road Map has very clear and strong connections to these academic standards, and each of the grade-level topics was derived from the mapping of the standards to ensure alignment among topics, challenges or problems, and the required academic standards for students. Therefore, the curriculum series takes a standards-based approach and is designed to provide authentic contexts for application of required knowledge and skills.

THEMES IN THE *STEM ROAD MAP CURRICULUM SERIES*

The K–12 STEM Road Map is organized around five real-world STEM themes that were generated through an examination of the big ideas and challenges for society included in STEM standards and those that are persistent dilemmas for current and future generations:

- Cause and Effect

- Innovation and Progress

- The Represented World

- Sustainable Systems

- Optimizing the Human Experience

These themes are designed as springboards for launching students into an exploration of real-world learning situated within big ideas. Most important, the five STEM Road Map themes serve as a framework for scaffolding STEM learning across the K–12 continuum.

The themes are distributed across the STEM disciplines so that they represent the big ideas in science (Cause and Effect; Sustainable Systems), technology (Innovation and Progress; Optimizing the Human Experience), engineering (Innovation and Progress; Sustainable Systems; Optimizing the Human Experience), and mathematics (The Represented World), as well as concepts and challenges in social studies and 21st century skills that are also excellent contexts for learning in English language arts. The process of developing themes began with the clustering of the *NGSS* performance expectations and the National Academy of Engineering's grand challenges for engineering, which led to the development of the challenge in each module and connections of the module activities to the *CCSS Mathematics* and *CCSS ELA* standards. We performed these mapping processes with large teams of experts and found that these five themes provided breadth, depth, and coherence to frame a high-quality STEM learning experience from kindergarten through 12th grade.

Cause and Effect

The concept of cause and effect is a powerful and pervasive notion in the STEM fields. It is the foundation of understanding how and why things happen as they do. Humans spend considerable effort and resources trying to understand the causes and effects of natural and designed phenomena to gain better control over events and the environment and to be prepared to react appropriately. Equipped with the knowledge of a specific cause-and-effect relationship, we can lead better lives or contribute to the community by altering the cause, leading to a different effect. For example, if a person recognizes that irresponsible energy consumption leads to global climate change, that person can act to remedy his or her contribution to the situation. Although cause and effect is a core idea in the STEM fields, it can actually be difficult to determine. Students should be capable of understanding not only when evidence points to cause and effect but also when evidence points to relationships but not direct causality. The major goal of education is to foster students to be empowered, analytic thinkers, capable of thinking through complex processes to make important decisions. Understanding causality, as well as when it cannot be determined, will help students become better consumers, global citizens, and community members.

Innovation and Progress

One of the most important factors in determining whether humans will have a positive future is innovation. Innovation is the driving force behind progress, which helps create possibilities that did not exist before. Innovation and progress are creative entities, but in the STEM fields, they are anchored by evidence and logic, and they use established concepts to move the STEM fields forward. In creating something new, students must consider what is already known in the STEM fields and apply this knowledge appropriately. When we innovate, we create value that was not there previously and create new conditions and possibilities for even more innovations. Students should consider how their innovations might affect progress and use their STEM thinking to change current human burdens to benefits. For example, if we develop more efficient cars that use by-products from another manufacturing industry, such as food processing, then we have used waste productively and reduced the need for the waste to be hauled away, an indirect benefit of the innovation.

The Represented World

When we communicate about the world we live in, how the world works, and how we can meet the needs of humans, sometimes we can use the actual phenomena to explain a concept. Sometimes, however, the concept is too big, too slow, too small, too fast, or too complex for us to explain using the actual phenomena, and we must use a representation or a model to help communicate the important features. We need representations and models such as graphs, tables, mathematical expressions, and diagrams because it makes our thinking visible. For example, when examining geologic time, we cannot actually observe the passage of such large chunks of time, so we create a timeline or a model that uses a proportional scale to visually illustrate how much time has passed for different eras. Another example may be something too complex for students at a particular grade level, such as explaining the p subshell orbitals of electrons to fifth graders. Instead, we use the Bohr model, which more closely represents the orbiting of planets and is accessible to fifth graders.

When we create models, they are helpful because they point out the most important features of a phenomenon. We also create representations of the world with mathematical functions, which help us change parameters to suit the situation. Creating representations of a phenomenon engages students because they are able to identify the important features of that phenomenon and communicate them directly. But because models are estimates of a phenomenon, they leave out some of the details, so it is important for students to evaluate their usefulness as well as their shortcomings.

Sustainable Systems

From an engineering perspective, the term *system* refers to the use of "concepts of component need, component interaction, systems interaction, and feedback. The interaction of subcomponents to produce a functional system is a common lens used by all engineering disciplines for understanding, analysis, and design." (Koehler, Bloom, and Binns 2013, p. 8). Systems can be either open (e.g., an ecosystem) or closed (e.g., a car battery). Ideally, a system should be sustainable, able to maintain equilibrium without much energy from outside the structure. Looking at a garden, we see flowers blooming, weeds sprouting, insects buzzing, and various forms of life living within its boundaries. This is an example of an ecosystem, a collection of living organisms that survive together, functioning as a system. The interaction of the organisms within the system and the influences of the environment (e.g., water, sunlight) can maintain the system for a period of time, thus demonstrating its ability to endure. Sustainability is a desirable feature of a system because it allows for existence of the entity in the long term.

In the STEM Road Map project, we identified different standards that we consider to be oriented toward systems that students should know and understand in the K–12 setting. These include ecosystems, the rock cycle, Earth processes (such as erosion, tectonics, ocean currents, weather phenomena), Earth-Sun-Moon cycles, heat transfer, and the interaction among the geosphere, biosphere, hydrosphere, and atmosphere. Students and teachers should understand that we live in a world of systems that are not independent of each other, but rather are intrinsically linked such that a disruption in one part of a system will have reverberating effects on other parts of the system.

Optimizing the Human Experience

Science, technology, engineering, and mathematics as disciplines have the capacity to continuously improve the ways humans live, interact, and find meaning in the world, thus working to optimize the human experience. This idea has two components: being more suited to our environment and being more fully human. For example, the progression of STEM ideas can help humans create solutions to complex problems, such as improving ways to access water sources, designing energy sources with minimal impact on our environment, developing new ways of communication and expression, and building efficient shelters. STEM ideas can also provide access to the secrets and wonders of nature. Learning in STEM requires students to think logically and systematically, which is a way of knowing the world that is markedly different from knowing the world as an artist. When students can employ various ways of knowing and understand when it is appropriate to use a different way of knowing or integrate ways of knowing, they are fully experiencing the best of what it is to be human. The problem-based learning scenarios provided in the STEM Road Map help students develop ways of thinking like STEM professionals as they ask questions and design solutions. They learn to optimize the human experience by innovating improvements in the designed world in which they live.

THE NEED FOR AN INTEGRATED STEM APPROACH

At a basic level, STEM stands for science, technology, engineering, and mathematics. Over the past decade, however, STEM has evolved to have a much broader scope and implications. Now, educators and policy makers refer to STEM as not only a concentrated area for investing in the future of the United States and other nations but also as a domain and mechanism for educational reform. The good intentions of the recent decade-plus of focus on accountability and increased testing has resulted in significant decreases not only in instructional time for teaching science and social studies but also in the flexibility of teachers to promote authentic, problem solving–focused classroom environments. The shift has had a detrimental impact on student acquisition of vitally important skills, which many refer to as 21st century skills, and often the ability of students to "think." Further, schooling has become increasingly siloed into compartments of mathematics, science, English language, arts and social studies, lacking any of the

connections that are overwhelmingly present in the real world around children. Students have experienced school as content provided in boxes that must be memorized, devoid of any real-world context, and often have little understanding of why they are learning these things.

STEM-focused projects, curriculum, activities, and schools have emerged as a means to address these challenges. However, most of these efforts have continued to focus on the individual STEM disciplines (predominantly science and engineering) through more STEM classes and after-school programs in a "STEM enhanced" approach (Breiner et al. 2012). But in traditional and STEM enhanced approaches, there is little to no focus on other disciplines that are integral to the context of STEM in the real world. Integrated STEM education, on the other hand, infuses the learning of important STEM content and concepts with a much-needed emphasis on 21st century skills and a problem- and project-based pedagogy that more closely mirrors the real-world setting for society's challenges. It incorporates social studies, English language arts, and the arts as pivotal and necessary (Johnson 2013; Rennie, Venville, and Wallace 2012; Roehrig et al. 2012).

Framework for Stem Integration in The Classroom

The *STEM Road Map Curriculum Series* is grounded in the Framework for STEM Integration in the Classroom as conceptualized by Moore, Guzey, and Brown (2014) and Moore et al. (2014). The framework has six elements, described in the context of how they are used in the *STEM Road Map Curriculum Series* as follows:

1. The STEM Road Map contexts are meaningful to students and provide motivation to engage with the content. Together, these allow students to have different ways to enter into the challenge.

2. The STEM Road Map modules include engineering design that allows students to design technologies (i.e., products that are part of the designed world) for a compelling purpose.

3. The STEM Road Map modules provide students with the opportunities to learn from failure and redesign based on the lessons learned.

4. The STEM Road Map modules include standards-based disciplinary content as the learning objectives.

5. The STEM Road Map modules include student-centered pedagogies that allow students to grapple with the content, tie their ideas to the context, and learn to think for themselves as they deepen their conceptual knowledge.

6. The STEM Road Map modules emphasize 21st century skills and, in particular, highlight communication and teamwork.

All of the STEM Road Map modules incorporate these six elements; however, the level of emphasis on each of these elements varies based on the challenge or problem in each module.

THE NEED FOR THE *STEM ROAD MAP CURRICULUM SERIES*

As focus is increasing on integrated STEM, and additional schools and programs decide to move their curriculum and instruction in this direction, there is a need for high-quality, research-based curriculum designed with integrated STEM at the core. Several good resources are available to help teachers infuse engineering or more STEM enhanced approaches, but no curriculum exists that spans K–12 with an integrated STEM focus. The next chapter provides detailed information about the specific pedagogy, instructional strategies, and learning theory on which the *STEM Road Map Curriculum Series* is grounded.

REFERENCES

Breiner, J., M. Harkness, C. C. Johnson, and C. Koehler. 2012. What is STEM? A discussion about conceptions of STEM in education and partnerships. *School Science and Mathematics* 112 (1): 3–11.

Johnson, C. C. 2013. Conceptualizing integrated STEM education: Editorial. *School Science and Mathematics* 113 (8): 367–368.

Koehler, C. M., M. A. Bloom, and I. C. Binns. 2013. Lights, camera, action: Developing a methodology to document mainstream films' portrayal of nature of science and scientific inquiry. *Electronic Journal of Science Education* 17 (2).

Moore, T. J., S. S. Guzey, and A. Brown. 2014. Greenhouse design to increase habitable land: An engineering unit. *Science Scope* 51–57.

Moore, T. J., M. S. Stohlmann, H.-H. Wang, K. M. Tank, A. W. Glancy, and G. H. Roehrig. 2014. Implementation and integration of engineering in K–12 STEM education. In *Engineering in pre-college settings: Synthesizing research, policy, and practices,* ed. S. Purzer, J. Strobel, and M. Cardella, 35–60. West Lafayette, IN: Purdue Press.

Rennie, L., G. Venville, and J. Wallace. 2012. *Integrating science, technology, engineering, and mathematics: Issues, reflections, and ways forward.* New York: Routledge.

Roehrig, G. H., T. J. Moore, H. H. Wang, and M. S. Park. 2012. Is adding the E enough? Investigating the impact of K–12 engineering standards on the implementation of STEM integration. *School Science and Mathematics* 112 (1): 31–44.

STRATEGIES USED IN THE *STEM ROAD MAP CURRICULUM SERIES*

Erin E. Peters-Burton, Carla C. Johnson, Toni A. May, and Tamara J. Moore

The *STEM Road Map Curriculum Series* uses what has been identified through research as best-practice pedagogy, including embedded formative assessment strategies throughout each module. This chapter briefly describes the key strategies that are employed in the series.

PROJECT- AND PROBLEM-BASED LEARNING

Each module in the *STEM Road Map Curriculum Series* uses either project-based learning or problem-based learning to drive the instruction. Project-based learning begins with a driving question to guide student teams in addressing a contextualized local or community problem or issue. The outcome of project-based instruction is a product that is conceptualized, designed, and tested through a series of scaffolded learning experiences (Blumenfeld et al. 1991; Krajcik and Blumenfeld 2006). Problem-based learning is often grounded in a fictitious scenario, challenge, or problem (Barell 2006; Lambros 2004). On the first day of instruction within the unit, student teams are provided with the context of the problem. Teams work through a series of activities and use open-ended research to develop their potential solution to the problem or challenge, which need not be a tangible product (Johnson 2003).

ENGINEERING DESIGN PROCESS

The *STEM Road Map Curriculum Series* uses engineering design as a way to facilitate integrated STEM within the modules. The engineering design process (EDP) is depicted in Figure 2.1 (p. 10). It highlights two major aspects of engineering design – problem scoping and solution generation – and six specific components of

DOI: 10.4324/9781003261711-3

Figure 2.1. Engineering Design Process

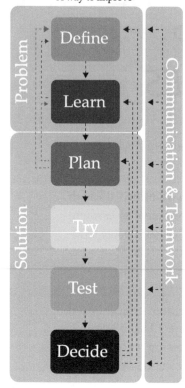

Copyright © 2015 PictureSTEM-Purdue University Research Foundation

working toward a design: define the problem, learn about the problem, plan a solution, try the solution, test the solution, decide whether the solution is good enough. It also shows that communication and teamwork are involved throughout the entire process. As the arrows in the figure indicate, the order in which the components of engineering design are addressed depends on what becomes needed as designers progress through the EDP. Designers must communicate and work in teams throughout the process. The EDP is iterative, meaning that components of the process can be repeated as needed until the design is good enough to present to the client as a potential solution to the problem.

Problem scoping is the process of gathering and analyzing information to deeply understand the engineering design problem. It includes defining the problem and learning about the problem. Defining the problem includes identifying the problem, the client, and the end user of the design. The client is the person (or people) who hired the designers to do the work, and the end user is the person (or people) who will use the final design. The designers must also identify the criteria and the constraints of the problem. The criteria are the things the client wants from the solution, and the constraints are the things that limit the possible solutions. The designers must spend significant time learning about the problem, which can include activities such as the following:

- Reading informational texts and researching about relevant concepts or contexts

- Identifying and learning about needed mathematical and scientific skills, knowledge, and tools

- Learning about things done previously to solve similar problems

- Experimenting with possible materials that could be used in the design

Problem scoping also allows designers to consider how to measure the success of the design in addressing specific criteria and staying within the constraints over multiple iterations of solution generation.

Solution generation includes planning a solution, trying the solution, testing the solution, and deciding whether the solution is good enough. Planning the solution includes generating many design ideas that both address the criteria and meet the constraints.

Here the designers must consider what was learned about the problem during problem scoping. Design plans include clear communication of design ideas through media such as notebooks, blueprints, schematics, or storyboards. They also include details about the design, such as measurements, materials, colors, costs of materials, instructions for how things fit together, and sets of directions. Making the decision about which design idea to move forward involves considering the trade-offs of each design idea.

Once a clear design plan is in place, the designers must try the solution. Trying the solution includes developing a prototype (a testable model) based on the plan generated. The prototype might be something physical or a process to accomplish a goal. This component of design requires that the designers consider the risk involved in implementing the design. The prototype developed must be tested. Testing the solution includes conducting fair tests that verify whether the plan is a solution that is good enough to meet the client and end user needs and wants. Data need to be collected about the results of the tests of the prototype, and these data should be used to make evidence-based decisions regarding the design choices made in the plan. Here, the designers must again consider the criteria and constraints for the problem.

Using the data gathered from the testing, the designers must decide whether the solution is good enough to meet the client and end user needs and wants by assessment based on the criteria and constraints. Here, the designers must justify or reject design decisions based on the background research gathered while learning about the problem and on the evidence gathered during the testing of the solution. The designers must now decide whether to present the current solution to the client as a possibility or to do more iterations of design on the solution. If they decide that improvements need to be made to the solution, the designers must decide if there is more that needs to be understood about the problem, client, or end user; if another design idea should be tried; or if more planning needs to be conducted on the same design. One way or another, more work needs to be done.

Throughout the process of designing a solution to meet a client's needs and wants, designers work in teams and must communicate to each other, the client, and likely the end user. Teamwork is important in engineering design because multiple perspectives and differing skills and knowledge are valuable when working to solve problems. Communication is key to the success of the designed solution. Designers must communicate their ideas clearly using many different representations, such as text in an engineering notebook, diagrams, flowcharts, technical briefs, or memos to the client.

LEARNING CYCLE

The same format for the learning cycle is used in all grade levels throughout the STEM Road Map, so that students engage in a variety of activities to learn about phenomena in the modules thoroughly and have consistent experiences in the problem- and project-based learning modules. Expectations for learning by younger students are

not as high as for older students, but the format of the progression of learning is the same. Students who have learned with curriculum from the STEM Road Map in early grades know what to expect in later grades. The learning cycle consists of five parts – Introductory Activity/Engagement, Activity/Exploration, Explanation, Elaboration/ Application of Knowledge, and Evaluation/Assessment – and is based on the empirically tested 5E model from BSCS (Bybee et al. 2006).

In the Introductory Activity/Engagement phase, teachers introduce the module challenge and use a unique approach designed to pique students' curiosity. This phase gets students to start thinking about what they already know about the topic and begin wondering about key ideas. The Introductory Activity/Engagement phase positions students to be confident about what they are about to learn, because they have prior knowledge, and clues them into what they don't yet know.

In the Activity/Exploration phase, the teacher sets up activities in which students experience a deeper look at the topics that were introduced earlier. Students engage in the activities and generate new questions or consider possibilities using preliminary investigations. Students work independently, in small groups, and in whole-group settings to conduct investigations, resulting in common experiences about the topic and skills involved in the real-world activities. Teachers can assess students' development of concepts and skills based on the common experiences during this phase.

During the Explanation phase, teachers direct students' attention to concepts they need to understand and skills they need to possess to accomplish the challenge. Students participate in activities to demonstrate their knowledge and skills to this point, and teachers can pinpoint gaps in student knowledge during this phase.

In the Elaboration/Application of Knowledge phase, teachers present students with activities that engage in higher-order thinking to create depth and breadth of student knowledge, while connecting ideas across topics within and across STEM. Students apply what they have learned thus far in the module to a new context or elaborate on what they have learned about the topic to a deeper level of detail.

In the last phase, Evaluation/Assessment, teachers give students summative feedback on their knowledge and skills as demonstrated through the challenge. This is not the only point of assessment (as discussed in the section on Embedded Formative Assessments), but it is an assessment of the culmination of the knowledge and skills for the module. Students demonstrate their cognitive growth at this point and reflect on how far they have come since the beginning of the module. The challenges are designed to be multidimensional in the ways students must collaborate and communicate their new knowledge.

STEM RESEARCH NOTEBOOK

One of the main components of the *STEM Road Map Curriculum Series* is the STEM Research Notebook, a place for students to capture their ideas, questions, observations, reflections, evidence of progress, and other items associated with their daily work. At the beginning of each module, the teacher walks students through the setup of the STEM Research Notebook, which could be a three-ring binder, composition book, or spiral notebook. You may wish to have students create divided sections so that they can easily access work from various disciplines during the module. Electronic notebooks kept on student devices are also acceptable and encouraged. Students will develop their own table of contents and create chapters in the notebook for each module.

Each lesson in the *STEM Road Map Curriculum Series* includes one or more prompts that are designed for inclusion in the STEM Research Notebook and appear as questions or statements that the teacher assigns to students. These prompts require students to apply what they have learned across the lesson to solve the big problem or challenge for that module. Each lesson is designed to meaningfully refer students to the larger problem or challenge they have been assigned to solve with their teams. The STEM Research Notebook is designed to be a key formative assessment tool, as students' daily entries provide evidence of what they are learning. The notebook can be used as a mechanism for dialogue between the teacher and students, as well as for peer and self-evaluation.

The use of the STEM Research Notebook is designed to scaffold student notebooking skills across the grade bands in the *STEM Road Map Curriculum Series*. In the early grades, children learn how to organize their daily work in the notebook as a way to collect their products for future reference. In elementary school, students structure their notebooks to integrate background research along with their daily work and lesson prompts. In the upper grades (middle and high school), students expand their use of research and data gathering through team discussions to more closely mirror the work of STEM experts in the real world.

THE ROLE OF ASSESSMENT IN THE *STEM ROAD MAP CURRICULUM SERIES*

Starting in the middle years and continuing into secondary education, the word *assessment* typically brings grades to mind. These grades may take the form of a letter or a percentage, but they typically are used as a representation of a student's content mastery. If well thought out and implemented, however, classroom assessment can offer teachers, parents, and students valuable information about student learning and misconceptions that does not necessarily come in the form of a grade (Popham 2013).

The *STEM Road Map Curriculum Series* provides a set of assessments for each module. Teachers are encouraged to use assessment information for more than just assigning grades to students. Instead, assessments of activities requiring students to actively engage in their learning, such as student journaling in STEM Research Notebooks, collaborative presentations, and constructing graphic organizers, should be used to move student learning forward. Whereas other curriculum with assessments may include

objective-type (multiple-choice or matching) tests, quizzes, or worksheets, we have intentionally avoided these forms of assessments to better align assessment strategies with teacher instruction and student learning techniques. Since the focus of this book is on project- or problem-based STEM curriculum and instruction that focuses on higher-level thinking skills, appropriate and authentic performance assessments were developed to elicit the most reliable and valid indication of growth in student abilities (Brookhart and Nitko 2008).

Comprehensive Assessment System

Assessment throughout all STEM Road Map curriculum modules acts as a comprehensive system in which formative and summative assessments work together to provide teachers with high-quality information on student learning. Formative assessment occurs when the teacher finds out formally or informally what a student knows about a smaller, defined concept or skill and provides timely feedback to the student about his or her level of proficiency. Summative assessments occur when students have performed all activities in the module and are given a cumulative performance evaluation in which they demonstrate their growth in learning.

A comprehensive assessment system can be thought of as akin to a sporting event. Formative assessments are the practices: It is important to accomplish them consistently, they provide feedback to help students improve their learning, and making mistakes can be worthwhile if students are given an opportunity to learn from them. Summative assessments are the competitions: Students need to be prepared to perform at the best of their ability. Without multiple opportunities to practice skills along the way through formative assessments, students will not have the best chance of demonstrating growth in abilities through summative assessments (Black and Wiliam 1998).

Embedded Formative Assessments

Formative assessments in this module serve two main purposes: to provide feedback to students about their learning and to provide important information for the teacher to inform immediate instructional needs. Providing feedback to students is particularly important when conducting problem- or project-based learning because students take on much of the responsibility for learning, and teachers must facilitate student learning in an informed way. For example, if students are required to conduct research for the Activity/Exploration phase but are not familiar with what constitutes a reliable resource, they may develop misconceptions based on poor information. When a teacher monitors this learning through formative assessments and provides specific feedback related to the instructional goals, students are less likely to develop incomplete or incorrect conceptions in their independent investigations. By using formative assessment to detect problems in student learning and then acting on this information, teachers help move student learning forward through these teachable moments.

Formative assessments come in a variety of formats. They can be informal, such as asking students probing questions related to student knowledge or tasks or simply observing students engaged in an activity to gather information about student skills. Formative assessments can also be formal, such as a written quiz or a laboratory practical.

Regardless of the type, three key steps must be completed when using formative assessments (Sondergeld, Bell, and Leusner 2010). First, the assessment is delivered to students so that teachers can collect data. Next, teachers analyze the data (student responses) to determine student strengths and areas that need additional support. Finally, teachers use the results from information collected to modify lessons and create learning environments that reinforce weak points in student learning. If student learning information is not used to modify instruction, the assessment cannot be considered formative in nature. Formative assessments can be about content, science process skills, or even learning skills. When a formative assessment focuses on content, it assesses student knowledge about the disciplinary core ideas from the *Next Generation Science Standards* (*NGSS*) or content objectives from *Common Core State Standards for Mathematics* (*CCSS Mathematics*) or *Common Core State Standards for English Language Arts* (*CCSS ELA*). Content-focused formative assessments ask students questions about declarative knowledge regarding the concepts they have been learning. Process skills formative assessments examine the extent to which a student can perform science and engineering practices from the *NGSS* or process objectives from *CCSS Mathematics* or *CCSS ELA*, such as constructing an argument. Learning skills can also be assessed formatively by asking students to reflect on the ways they learn best during a module and identify ways they could have learned more.

Assessment Maps

Assessment maps or blueprints can be used to ensure alignment between classroom instruction and assessment. If what students are learning in the classroom is not the same as the content on which they are assessed, the resultant judgment made on student learning will be invalid (Brookhart and Nitko 2008). Therefore, the issue of instruction and assessment alignment is critical. The assessment map for this book (found in Chapter 3) indicates by lesson whether the assessment should be completed as a group or on an individual basis, identifies the assessment as formative or summative in nature, and aligns the assessment with its corresponding learning objectives.

Note that the module includes far more formative assessments than summative assessments. This is done intentionally to provide students with multiple opportunities to practice their learning of new skills before completing a summative assessment. Note also that formative assessments are used to collect information on only one or two learning objectives at a time so that potential relearning or instructional modifications can focus on smaller and more manageable chunks of information. Conversely,

summative assessments in the module cover many more learning objectives, as they are traditionally used as final markers of student learning. This is not to say that information collected from summative assessments cannot or should not be used formatively. If teachers find that gaps in student learning persist after a summative assessment is completed, it is important to revisit these existing misconceptions or areas of weakness before moving on (Black et al. 2003).

SELF-REGULATED LEARNING THEORY IN THE STEM ROAD MAP MODULES

Many learning theories are compatible with the STEM Road Map modules, such as constructivism, situated cognition, and meaningful learning. However, we feel that the self-regulated learning theory (SRL) aligns most appropriately (Zimmerman 2000). SRL requires students to understand that thinking needs to be motivated and managed (Ritchhart, Church, and Morrison 2011). The STEM Road Map modules are student centered and are designed to provide students with choices, concrete hands-on experiences, and opportunities to see and make connections, especially across subjects (Eliason and Jenkins 2012; NAEYC 2016). Additionally, SRL is compatible with the modules because it fosters a learning environment that supports students' motivation, enables students to become aware of their own learning strategies, and requires reflection on learning while experiencing the module (Peters and Kitsantas 2010).

The theory behind SRL (see Figure 2.2) explains the different processes that students engage in before, during, and after a learning task. Because SRL is a cyclical learning process, the accomplishment of one cycle develops strategies for the next learning cycle. This cyclic way of learning aligns with the various sections in the STEM Road Map lesson plans on Introductory Activity/ Engagement, Activity/ Exploration, Explanation, Elaboration/Application of Knowledge, and Evaluation/Assessment. Since the students engaged in a module take on much of the responsibility for learning, this theory also provides guidance for teachers to keep students on the right track.

Figure 2.2. SRL Theory

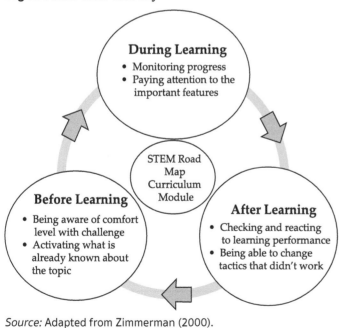

Source: Adapted from Zimmerman (2000).

Table 2.1. SRL Learning Process Components

Learning Process Components	Example from Rebuilding the Natural Environment Module	Lesson Number
Before Learning		
Motivates students	Students brainstorm their own experiences with energy consumption.	Lesson 1
Evokes prior learning	Students will discuss their understanding of electricity generation within teams and share their ideas with the class. Students will be asked to give their responses on the following questions: (a) What is electricity? (b) How is it generated? (c) How does it get to our houses?	Lesson 1
During Learning		
Focuses on important features	Students must determine the cost-effectiveness of taking a single-family home off the current electrical grid and powering it solely from available renewable/sustainable energy sources. Students will need to research the energy output of devices, use weather data to accurately estimate the amount of time each device will be able to generate electricity (amount of sunlight per day and season for solar, average amount of wind per day and season for wind, etc.), and conservatively calculate the kilowatt hours generated on average for a whole-home system.	Lesson 3
Helps students monitor their progress	Teacher monitors student STEM Research Notebooks for the accuracy of each device and for how the devices work as a system.	Lesson 3
After Learning		
Evaluates learning	Students receive feedback on the rubric for their innovation for their group work and for their individual work.	Lesson 4
Takes account of what worked and what did not work	Students will write a reflection on the quality of their work given feedback from the class and teacher.	Lesson 4

The remainder of this section explains how SRL theory is embedded within the five sections of each module and points out ways to support students in becoming independent learners of STEM while productively functioning in collaborative teams.

Before Learning: Setting the Stage

Before attempting a learning task such as the STEM Road Map modules, teachers should develop an understanding of their students' level of comfort with the process of accomplishing the learning and determine what they already know about the topic. When students are comfortable with attempting a learning task, they tend to take more risks in learning and as a result achieve deeper learning (Bandura 1986).

The STEM Road Map curriculum modules are designed to foster excitement from the very beginning. Each module has an Introductory Activity/Engagement section that introduces the overall topic from a unique and exciting perspective, engaging the students to learn more so that they can accomplish the challenge. The Introductory Activity also has a design component that helps teachers assess what students already know about the topic of the module. In addition to the deliberate designs in the lesson plans to support SRL, teachers can support a high level of student comfort with the learning challenge by finding out if students have ever accomplished the same kind of task and, if so, asking them to share what worked well for them.

During Learning: Staying the Course

Some students fear inquiry learning because they aren't sure what to do to be successful (Peters 2010). However, the STEM Road Map curriculum modules are embedded with tools to help students pay attention to knowledge and skills that are important for the learning task and to check student understanding along the way. One of the most important processes for learning is the ability for learners to monitor their own progress while performing a learning task (Peters 2012). The modules allow students to monitor their progress with tools such as the STEM Research Notebooks, in which they record what they know and can check whether they have acquired a complete set of knowledge and skills. The STEM Road Map modules support inquiry strategies that include previewing, questioning, predicting, clarifying, observing, discussing, and journaling (Morrison and Milner 2014). Through the use of technology throughout the modules, inquiry is supported by providing students access to resources and data while enabling them to process information, report the findings, collaborate, and develop 21st century skills.

It is important for teachers to encourage students to have an open mind about alternative solutions and procedures (Milner and Sondergeld 2015) when working through the STEM Road Map curriculum modules. Novice learners can have difficulty knowing what to pay attention to and tend to treat each possible avenue for information as equal (Benner 1984). Teachers are the mentors in a classroom and can point out ways for students to approach learning during the Activity/Exploration, Explanation, and Elaboration/Application of Knowledge portions of the lesson plans to ensure that students pay attention to the important concepts and skills throughout the module. For example, if a student is to demonstrate conceptual awareness of motion when working on roller coaster research, but the student has misconceptions about motion, the teacher can step in and redirect student learning.

After Learning: Knowing What Works

The classroom is a busy place, and it may often seem that there is no time for self-reflection on learning. Although skipping this reflective process may save time in the short term, it reduces the ability to take into account things that worked well and things that didn't so that teaching the module may be improved next time. In the long run, SRL skills are critical for students to become independent learners who can adapt to new situations. By investing the time it takes to teach students SRL skills, teachers can save time later, because students will be able to apply methods and approaches for learning that they have found effective to new situations. In the Evaluation/Assessment portion of the STEM Road Map curriculum modules, as well as in the formative assessments throughout the modules, two processes in the after-learning phase are supported: evaluating one's own performance and accounting for ways to adapt tactics that didn't work well. Students have many opportunities to self-assess in formative assessments, both in groups and individually, using the rubrics provided in the modules.

The designs of the *NGSS* and *CCSS* allow for students to learn in diverse ways, and the STEM Road Map curriculum modules emphasize that students can use a variety of tactics to complete the learning process. For example, students can use STEM Research Notebooks to record what they have learned during the various research activities. Notebook entries might include putting objectives in students' own words, compiling their prior learning on the topic, documenting new learning, providing proof of what they learned, and reflecting on what they felt successful doing and what they felt they still needed to work on. Perhaps students didn't realize that they were supposed to connect what they already knew with what they learned. They could record this and would be prepared in the next learning task to begin connecting prior learning with new learning.

SAFETY IN STEM

Student safety is a primary consideration in all subjects but is an area of particular concern in science, where students may interact with unfamiliar tools and materials that may pose additional safety risks. It is important to implement safety practices within the context of STEM investigations, whether in a classroom laboratory or in the field.

When you keep safety in mind as a teacher, you avoid many potential issues with the lesson while also protecting your students.

STEM safety practices encompass things considered in the typical science classroom. Ensure that students are familiar with basic safety considerations, such as wearing protective equipment (e.g., safety glasses or goggles and latex-free gloves) and taking care with sharp objects, and know emergency exit procedures. Teachers should learn beforehand the locations of the safety eyewash, fume hood, fire extinguishers, and emergency shut-off switch in the classroom and how to use them. Also be aware of any school or district safety policies that are in place and apply those that align with the work being conducted in the lesson. It is important to review all safety procedures annually.

STEM investigations should always be supervised. Each lesson in the modules includes teacher guidelines for applicable safety procedures that should be followed. Before each investigation, teachers should go over these safety procedures with the student teams. Some STEM focus areas such as engineering require that students can demonstrate how to properly use equipment in the maker space before the teacher allows them to proceed with the lesson.

Information about classroom science safety, including a safety checklist for science classrooms, general lab safety recommendations, and links to other science safety resources, is available at the Council of State Science Supervisors (CSSS) website at *www.csss-science. org/safety.shtml*. The National Science Teaching Association (NSTA) provides a list of science rules and regulations, including standard operating procedures for lab safety, and a safety acknowledgment form for students and parents or guardians to sign. You can access these resources at *http://static.nsta.org/pdfs/SafetyIn-TheScienceClassroom.pdf*. In addition, NSTA's Safety in the Science Classroom web page (*www.nsta.org/safety*) has numerous links to safety resources, including papers written by the NSTA Safety Advisory Board.

Disclaimer: The safety precautions for each activity are based on use of the recommended materials and instructions, legal safety standards, and better professional practices. Using alternative materials or procedures for these activities may jeopardize the level of safety and therefore is at the user's own risk.

REFERENCES

Bandura, A. 1986. *Social foundations of thought and action: A social cognitive theory.* Englewood Cliffs, NJ: Prentice-Hall.

Barell, J. 2006. *Problem-based learning: An inquiry approach.* Thousand Oaks, CA: Corwin Press.

Benner, P. 1984. *From novice to expert: Excellence and power in clinical nursing practice.* Menlo Park, CA: Addison-Wesley Publishing Company.

Black, P., C. Harrison, C. Lee, B. Marshall, and D. Wiliam. 2003. *Assessment for learning: Putting it into practice.* Berkshire, UK: Open University Press.

Black, P., and D. Wiliam. 1998. Inside the black box: Raising standards through classroom assessment. *Phi Delta Kappan* 80 (2): 139–148.

Blumenfeld, P., E. Soloway, R. Marx, J. Krajcik, M. Guzdial, and A. Palincsar. 1991. Motivating project-based learning: Sustaining the doing, supporting learning. *Educational Psychologist* 26 (3): 369–398.

Brookhart, S. M., and A. J. Nitko. 2008. *Assessment and grading in classrooms.* Upper Saddle River, NJ: Pearson.

Bybee, R., J. Taylor, A. Gardner, P. Van Scotter, J. Carlson, A. Westbrook, and N. Landes. 2006. *The BSCS 5E instructional model: Origins and effectiveness.* http://science.education.nih.gov/ houseofreps. nsf/b82d55fa138783c2852572c9004f5566/$FILE/Appendix?D.pdf.

Eliason, C. F., and L. T. Jenkins. 2012. *A practical guide to early childhood curriculum.* 9th ed. New York: Merrill.

Johnson, C. 2003. Bioterrorism is real-world science: Inquiry-based simulation mirrors real life. *Science Scope* 27 (3): 19–23.

Krajcik, J., and P. Blumenfeld. 2006. Project-based learning. In *The Cambridge handbook of the learning sciences,* ed. R. Keith Sawyer, 317–334. New York: Cambridge University Press.

Lambros, A. 2004. *Problem-based learning in middle and high school classrooms: A teacher's guide to implementation.* Thousand Oaks, CA: Corwin Press.

Milner, A. R., and T. Sondergeld. 2015. Gifted urban middle school students: The inquiry continuum and the nature of science. *National Journal of Urban Education and Practice* 8 (3): 442–461.

Morrison, V., and A. R. Milner. 2014. Literacy in support of science: A closer look at cross-curricular instructional practice. *Michigan Reading Journal* 46 (2): 42–56.

National Association for the Education of Young Children (NAEYC). 2016. Developmentally appropriate practice position statements. www.naeyc.org/positionstatements/dap.

Peters, E. E. 2010. Shifting to a student-centered science classroom: An exploration of teacher and student changes in perceptions and practices. *Journal of Science Teacher Education* 21 (3): 329–349.

Peters, E. E. 2012. Developing content knowledge in students through explicit teaching of the nature of science: Influences of goal setting and self-monitoring. *Science and Education* 21 (6): 881–898.

Peters, E. E., and A. Kitsantas. 2010. The effect of nature of science metacognitive prompts on science students' content and nature of science knowledge, metacognition, and self-regulatory efficacy. *School Science and Mathematics* 110: 382–396.

Popham, W. J. 2013. *Classroom assessment: What teachers need to know.* 7th ed. Upper Saddle River, NJ: Pearson.

Ritchhart, R., M. Church, and K. Morrison. 2011. *Making thinking visible: How to promote engagement, understanding, and independence for all learners.* San Francisco, CA: Jossey-Bass.

Sondergeld, T. A., C. A. Bell, and D. M. Leusner. 2010. Understanding how teachers engage in formative assessment. *Teaching and Learning* 24 (2): 72–86.

Zimmerman, B. J. 2000. Attaining self-regulation: A social-cognitive perspective. In *Handbook of self-regulation*, ed. M. Boekaerts, P. Pintrich, and M. Zeidner, 13–39. San Diego: Academic Press.

PART 2

REBUILDING THE NATURAL ENVIRONMENT
STEM ROAD MAP MODULE

REBUILDING THE NATURAL ENVIRONMENT MODULE OVERVIEW

Bradley Rankin, Anthony Pellegrino, Erin E. Peters-Burton,
Jennifer Drake Patrick, Janet B. Walton, and Carla C. Johnson

THEME: Optimizing the Human Experience

LEAD DISCIPLINE: Science

MODULE SUMMARY

The inclusion of the category of "Green Economy Sector" in *The Occupations Online Data Base* (2014) is a strong indication that future businesses will need to consider not only their financial progress, but also their positive contributions to the human experience, including careers that focus on rebuilding the natural environment. In this module, students will connect to their prior knowledge about energy production and the effects of this process on the natural environment to create innovations in renewable sources of energy based on research evidence. Student teams are challenged to use skills from different academic disciplines to design an innovative way to meet society's energy needs and to develop a pitch to market their innovation, focusing on how the innovation will optimize human experiences while being mindful of the natural environment. Further, students will use predictive skills to consider how their innovation will affect energy consumption and what the implications of this consumption are over a long period of time. In effect, students will be thinking about how innovation can make the world a better place to live for humans, while finding ways to sustain progress and conserve resources. (adapted from E. Peters-Burton et al., 2015).

ESTABLISHED GOALS AND OBJECTIVES

At the conclusion of this module, students will be able to do the following:

- List several forms of renewable, sustainable energy sources.

- Apply their understanding of how alternators are used to generate electricity in lab experiments, as well as explain how tools such as windmills and dams are used to operate them.

- Describe how electricity is generated in photovoltaic cells.

- Calculate the amount of electricity consumed by several household items and consider this consumption when determining the average monthly energy consumption of households around the world in comparison to U.S. households.

- Differentiate a watt from a watt-hour and calculate the number of watt-hours a given energy source can generate.

- Understand how fossil fuels have been used in the production of electricity and the impact they have had on the world's economy, humans' quality of life, and the earth.

- Identify several hindrances to the creation of new energy sources as well as ideas to counter them.

- List several factors that can be used to motivate people from all walks of life to use renewable and sustainable energies.

- Create a fictional company that uses renewable energies.

CHALLENGE OR PROBLEM FOR STUDENTS TO SOLVE: ENERGY INNOVATION CHALLENGE

Student teams are challenged to act as renewable energy companies creating a cost-effective, innovative way to create energy. Each team will research current renewable sources of energy and then design and pitch an idea for an innovative renewable energy product. Teams will each create a model for the change their product can effect in energy consumption in the U.S. or globally.

CONTENT STANDARDS ADDRESSED IN THIS STEM ROAD MAP MODULE

A full listing with descriptions of the standards this module addresses can be found in the appendix. Listings of the particular standards addressed within lessons are provided in a table for each lesson in Chapter 4.

STEM RESEARCH NOTEBOOK

Each student should maintain a STEM Research Notebook, which will serve as a place for students to organize their work throughout this module (see p. 12 for more general

discussion on setup and use of the notebook). All written work in the module should be included in the notebook, including records of students' thoughts and ideas, fictional accounts based on the concepts in the module, and records of student progress through the EDP. The notebooks may be maintained across subject areas, giving students the opportunity to see that although their classes may be separated during the school day, the knowledge they gain is connected. You may also wish to have students include the STEM Research Notebook Guidelines student handout on p. 28 in their notebooks.

Emphasize to students the importance of organizing all information in a Research Notebook. Explain to them that scientists and other researchers maintain detailed Research Notebooks in their work. These notebooks, which are crucial to researchers' work because they contain critical information and track the researchers' progress, are often considered legal documents for scientists who are pursuing patents or wish to provide proof of their discovery process.

STUDENT HANDOUT

STEM RESEARCH NOTEBOOK GUIDELINES

STEM professionals record their ideas, inventions, experiments, questions, observations, and other work details in notebooks so that they can use these notebooks to help them think about their projects and the problems they are trying to solve. You will each keep a STEM Research Notebook during this module that is like the notebooks that STEM professionals use. In this notebook, you will include all your work and notes about ideas you have. The notebook will help you connect your daily work with the big problem or challenge you are working to solve.

It is important that you organize your notebook entries under the following headings:

1. **Chapter Topic or Title of Problem or Challenge:** You will start a new chapter in your STEM Research Notebook for each new module. This heading is the topic or title of the big problem or challenge that your team is working to solve in this module.

2. **Date and Topic of Lesson Activity for the Day:** Each day, you will begin your daily entry by writing the date and the day's lesson topic at the top of a new page. Write the page number both on the page and in the table of contents.

3. **Information Gathered from Research:** This is information you find from outside resources such as websites or books.

4. **Information Gained from Class or Discussions with Team Members:** This information includes any notes you take in class and notes about things your team discusses. You can include drawings of your ideas here, too.

5. **New Data Collected from Investigations:** This includes data gathered from experiments, investigations, and activities in class.

6. **Documents:** These are handouts and other resources you may receive in class that will help you solve your big problem or challenge. Paste or staple these documents in your STEM Research Notebook for safekeeping and easy access later.

7. **Personal Reflections:** Here, you record your own thoughts and ideas on what you are learning.

8. **Lesson Prompts:** These are questions or statements that your teacher assigns you within each lesson to help you solve your big problem or challenge. You will respond to the prompts in your notebook.

9. **Other Items:** This section includes any other items your teacher gives you or other ideas or questions you may have.

MODULE LAUNCH

To activate prior student knowledge and initiate discussion about energy sources, show students images of high altitude wind turbines and have students share their ideas about what they are and their experiences with seeing these types of turbines. Next, show students a video clip about high altitude wind turbines such as *www.youtube.com/watch?v=kldA4nWANA8*. Hold a class discussion about wind turbines as an alternative to fossil fuels for energy production, eliciting responses and/or opinions from students about why countries all over the world are pursuing technologies such as high-altitude wind turbines. Have students share their ideas about the advantages and the disadvantages of using fossil fuels such as coal to produce energy. Focus students' attention on the non-renewability of fossil fuels and prompt discussion about alternative energy sources. Tell students that in this module they will be challenged to work in teams to create energy companies that create and market innovative ways to create energy.

PREREQUISITE SKILLS FOR THE MODULE

Students enter this module with a wide range of preexisting skills, information, and knowledge. Table 3.1 provides an overview of prerequisite skills and knowledge that students are expected to apply in this module, along with examples of how they apply this knowledge throughout the module. Differentiation strategies are also provided for students who may need additional support in acquiring or applying this knowledge.

Table 3.1. Prerequisite Key Knowledge and Examples of Applications and Differentiation Strategies

Prerequisite key knowledge	Application of knowledge	Differentiation for students needing knowledge
Energy and Electricity Understand that society uses energy that is produced from a variety of sources that can be categorized as primary sources (fossil fuels, nuclear energy, and renewable energy) and secondary sources (electricity) that are generated from primary sources. Understand that energy sources can be classified as renewable (naturally replenish themselves in relatively short periods of time) or nonrenewable (do not replenish themselves within short periods of time). Understand that electricity is the flow of electric charge from one place to another.	Students will extend their basic knowledge of electricity to how it is *generated* in turbines, batteries, and photovoltaic cells.	Students needing support understanding how electricity works may watch a video explaining the basics of electricity such as *Electricity 101 – Electricity Generation* found at *www.youtube.com/watch?v=20Vb6hlLQSgor* Teachers can review the basics of energy sources and electricity with students.

Continued

Table 3.1. (*Continued*)

Prerequisite key knowledge	Application of knowledge	Differentiation for students needing knowledge
Mathematics Be able to manipulate basic algebraic formulas and convert units.	Students will manipulate formulas dealing with energy production. Specifically, they will be able to calculate the amount of energy (watts) needed to power a particular appliance (or other household device) and the number of kilowatt-hours each device uses per month.	Teachers can work through energy formulas as a class and have students work individually to apply energy formulas and convert energy units. Teachers can provide examples of power bills and model and provide opportunities for students to calculate a power bill.

POTENTIAL STEM MISCONCEPTIONS

Students enter the classroom with a wide variety of prior knowledge and ideas, so it is important to be alert to misconceptions, or inappropriate understandings of foundational knowledge. These misconceptions can be classified as one of several types: "preconceived notions," opinions based on popular beliefs or understandings; "nonscientific beliefs," knowledge students have gained about science from sources outside the scientific community; "conceptual misunderstandings," incorrect conceptual models based on incomplete understanding of concepts; "vernacular misconceptions," misunderstandings of words based on their common use versus their scientific use; and "factual misconceptions," incorrect or imprecise knowledge learned in early life that remains unchallenged (NRC 1997, p. 28). Misconceptions must be addressed and dismantled in order for students to reconstruct their knowledge, and therefore teachers should be prepared to take the following steps:

- *Identify students' misconceptions.*

- *Provide a forum for students to confront their misconceptions.*

- *Help students reconstruct and internalize their knowledge, based on scientific models.* (NRC 1997, p. 29)

Keeley and Harrington (2010) recommend using diagnostic tools such as probes and formative assessment to identify and confront student misconceptions and begin the process of reconstructing student knowledge. Keeley and Harrington's *Uncovering Student Ideas in Science* series contains probes targeted toward uncovering student misconceptions in a variety of areas. In particular, Volume 1 of *Uncovering Student Ideas in Physical Science* (Keeley and Harrington 2010), about force/motion, may be useful resources for addressing student misconceptions in this module.

Some commonly held misconceptions specific to lesson content are provided with each lesson so that you can be alert for student misunderstanding of the science concepts presented and used during this module. The American Association for the Advancement of Science has also identified misconceptions that students frequently hold regarding various science concepts (see the links at *http://assessment.aaas.org/topics*).

SRL PROCESS COMPONENTS

Table 3.2 illustrates some of the activities in the Rebuilding the Natural Environment module and how they align to the SRL process before, during, and after learning.

Table 3.2. SRL Process Components

Learning Process Components	Example from Rebuilding the Natural Environment Module	Lesson Number
Before Learning		
Motivates students	Students brainstorm their own experiences with energy consumption.	Lesson 1
Evokes prior learning	Students will discuss their understanding of electricity generation within teams and share their ideas with the class. Students will be asked to give their responses on the following questions: (a) What is electricity? (b) How is it generated? (c) How does it get to our houses?	Lesson 1
During Learning		
Focuses on important features	Students must determine the cost-effectiveness of taking a single-family home off the current electrical grid and powering it solely from available renewable/sustainable energy sources. Students will need to research the energy output of devices, use weather data to accurately estimate the amount of time each device will be able to generate electricity (amount of sunlight per day and season for solar, average amount of wind per day and season for wind, etc.), and conservatively calculate the kilowatt hours generated on average for a whole-home system.	Lesson 3
Helps students monitor their progress	Teacher monitors student STEM Research Notebooks for the accuracy of each device and for how the devices work as a system.	Lesson 3
After Learning		
Evaluates learning	Students receive feedback on the rubric for their innovation for their group work and for their individual work.	Lesson 4
Takes account of what worked and what did not work	Students will write a reflection on the quality of their work given feedback from the class and teacher.	Lesson 4

STRATEGIES FOR DIFFERENTIATING INSTRUCTION WITHIN THIS MODULE

For the purposes of this curriculum module, differentiated instruction is conceptualized as a way to tailor instruction – including process, content, and product – to various student needs in your class. A number of differentiation strategies are integrated into lessons across the module. The problem- and project-based learning approach used in the lessons is designed to address students' multiple intelligences by providing a variety of entry points and methods to investigate the key concepts in the module (for example, investigating gardening from the perspectives of science and social issues via scientific inquiry, literature, journaling, and collaborative design). Differentiation strategies for students needing support in prerequisite knowledge can be found in Table 3.1 (p. 29). You are encouraged to use information gained about student prior knowledge during introductory activities and discussions to inform your instructional differentiation. Strategies incorporated into this lesson include flexible grouping, varied environmental learning contexts, assessments, compacting, tiered assignments and scaffolding.

Flexible Grouping: Students have the opportunity to learn in various contexts throughout the module, including alone, in groups, in quiet reading and research-oriented activities, and in active learning through inquiry and design activities. In addition, students learn in a variety of ways, including through doing inquiry activities, journaling, reading texts, watching videos, participating in class discussion, and conducting web-based research.

Varied Environmental Learning Contexts: Students have the opportunity to learn in various contexts throughout the module, including alone, in groups, in quiet reading and research-oriented activities, and in active learning through inquiry and design activities. In addition, students learn in a variety of ways, including through doing inquiry activities, journaling, reading a variety of texts, watching videos, participating in class discussion, and conducting web-based research.

Assessments: Students are assessed in a variety of ways throughout the module, including individual and collaborative formative and summative assessments. Students have the opportunity to produce work via written text, oral and media presentations, and modeling. You may choose to provide students with additional choices of media for their products (for example, PowerPoint presentations, posters, or student-created websites or blogs).

Compacting: Based on student prior knowledge, you may wish to adjust instructional activities for students who exhibit prior mastery of a learning objective. You may wish to compile a classroom database of research resources and supplementary readings for a variety of reading levels and on a variety of topics related to the module's topic to provide opportunities for students to undertake independent reading.

Tiered Assignments and Scaffolding: Based on your awareness of student ability, understanding of concepts, and mastery of skills, you may wish to provide students with variations on activities by adding complexity to assignments or providing more or fewer learning supports for activities throughout the module. For instance, some students may need additional support in identifying key search words and phrases for web-based research or may benefit from cloze sentence handouts to enhance vocabulary understanding. Other students may benefit from expanded reading selections and additional reflective writing or from working with manipulatives and other visual representations of mathematical concepts. You may also work with your school librarian to compile a set of topical resources at a variety of reading levels.

STRATEGIES FOR ENGLISH LANGUAGE LEARNERS

Students who are developing proficiency in English language skills require additional supports to simultaneously learn academic content and the specialized language associated with specific content areas. WIDA has created a framework for providing support to these students and makes available rubrics and guidance on differentiating instructional materials for English language learners (ELLs) (see *www.wida.us/get. aspx?id=7*). In particular, ELL students may benefit from additional sensory supports such as images, physical modeling, and graphic representations of module content, as well as interactive support through collaborative work. This module incorporates a variety of sensory supports and provides ongoing opportunities for ELL students to work collaboratively.

Teachers differentiating instruction for ELL students should carefully consider the needs of these students as they introduce and use academic language in various language domains (listening, speaking, reading, and writing) throughout this module. To adequately differentiate instruction for ELL students, teachers should have an understanding of the proficiency level of each student. The following five overarching 9–12 WIDA learning standards are relevant to this module:

Standard 1: Social and instructional language. Focus on social behavior in group work and class discussions.

Standard 2: The language of language arts. Focus on forms of print, elements of text, picture books, comprehension strategies, main ideas and details, persuasive language, creating informational text, and editing and revising.

Standard 3: The language of mathematics. Focus on numbers and operations, patterns, number sense, measurement, and strategies for problem solving.

Standard 4: The language of science. Focus on safety practices, energy sources, scientific process, and scientific inquiry.

Standard 5: The language of social studies. Focus on change from past to present, historical events, resources, transportation, map reading, and location of objects and places.

SAFETY CONSIDERATIONS FOR THE ACTIVITIES IN THIS MODULE

In this module, students create models variety of materials and should use caution when handling sharp objects and tools that can pinch. Students will also participate in investigations that involve electric current. Students should never touch any electrical equipment or circuits with wet hands and should never work with circuits near water. For more precautions, see the specific safety notes after the list of materials in each lesson. For more general safety guidelines, see the Safety in STEM section in Chapter 2 (p. 19).

DESIRED OUTCOMES AND MONITORING SUCCESS

The desired outcomes for this module are outlined in Table 3.3, along with suggested ways to gather evidence to monitor student success. For more specific details on desired outcomes, see the Established Goals and Objectives sections for the module and individual lessons.

Table 3.3. Desired Outcomes and Evidence of Success in Achieving Identified Outcomes

Desired Outcome	Evidence of Success in Achieving Identified Outcome	
Students will be able to identify several kinds of renewable/sustainable energy sources and calculate their electrical generation potential. They will understand the process that generates electricity and build a small-scale version of a renewable/sustainable energy source (hydro-electric, wind, etc.) for doing so. Furthermore, students will propose a design for an innovative device or system for generating enough electricity to eliminate the need for much of the fossil fuels used today.	**Performance Tasks** • Students maintain STEM Research Notebooks that contain designs, research notes, evidence of collaboration, and social studies and ELA-related work. • Students apply their understanding of energy sources to create models of renewable energy sources. • Students create essays about and present a renewable/sustainable energy source. • Students design innovative, renewable/sustainable energy products. • Students determine the environmental impact of their innovative products. • Students determine the economic impact of their products. • Students create advertisements for their products targeting several demographic groups. • Students are assessed using project rubrics that focus on content and application of skills related to academic content.	**Other Measures** • Students are able to effectively collaborate to complete tasks.

ASSESSMENT PLAN OVERVIEW AND MAP

Table 3.4 provides an overview of the major group and individual *products* and *deliverables*, or things that student teams will produce in this module, that constitute the assessment for this module. See Table 3.5 for a full assessment map of formative and summative assessments in this module.

Table 3.4. Major Products and Deliverables in Lead Disciplines for Groups and Individuals

Lesson	Major Group Products/Deliverables	Major Individual Products/ Deliverables
1	• Voltage, Amperage, and Ohms Investigation Designs and Results • Electric Generator Investigation Design and Results • Windmill, Waterway or Steam Turbine Prototype	• STEM Research Notebook Prompts • Review of Major Concepts Graphic Organizer • Windmill, Waterway or Steam Turbine Paper
2	• Photovoltaic Cell Investigation	• STEM Research Notebook Prompt • Paper on Sustainable/Renewable Energy Sources
3	• Design of Home Power System • Design of Brochures for two different demographic groups	• STEM Research Notebook Prompt
4	• Innovative and renewable/sustainable energy product or system (group rubric)	• Innovative and renewable/ sustainable energy product or system (individual rubric)

Table 3.5. Assessment Map for Car Crashes Module

Lesson	Assessment	Group/ Individual	Formative/ Summative	Lesson Objective Assessed
1	STEM Research Notebook *prompts*	Group	Formative	Understand how electricity is generated and transported.
1	STEM Research notebook *prompts*	Group	Formative	Understand how lack of electrical power impacts people.

Continued

Table 3.5. (*Continued*)

Lesson	Assessment	Group/ Individual	Formative/ Summative	Lesson Objective Assessed
1	STEM Research notebook *prompts*	Individual/ Group	Formative	Understand how electricity is generated and transported by different technologies.
1	Voltage, Amperage, and Ohms Investigation *design and results*	Group	Formative	Understand that elements have electrons moving freely between them and how this impacts amperes – current. Understand that resistors work in conjunction with voltage and amperes to create circuits.
1	Electric Generator Investigation *design and results*	Group	Formative	Understand the basics of the electro-magnetic force. Understand how electricity is generated and transported.
1	Review of Major Concepts *graphic organizer*	Individual/ Group	Formative	Define major terms and explain how they are used.
1	Windmill, Waterway or Steam Turbine *prototype and paper*	Group	Formative	Develop energy source prototype. Collect data on electricity measurements from the prototype. Do basic calculations involving volts and amperes. Write a paper detailing the electricity generation, electromagnetic process, and rate at which environmental issues impact the energy source.
2	STEM Research Notebook *prompts*	Individual	Formative	Explain how electrons are involved in powering a smartphone.
2	STEM Research Notebook *prompts*	Individual	Formative	Explain pros and cons of using renewable/ sustainable energy sources.
2	STEM Research Notebook *prompts*	Individual	Formative	Explain why solar panels are effective energy sources to people from various political party affiliations.
2	STEM Research Notebook *prompts*	Individual	Formative	Describe the basics of electricity generation in photovoltaic cells.

Continued

Table 3.5. (*Continued*)

Lesson	Assessment	Group/ Individual	Formative/ Summative	Lesson Objective Assessed
2	Paper on Sustainable/ Renewable Energy Sources *rubric*	Individual	Summative	Write in-depth analysis of how one form of renewable/sustainable energy works. Describe energy source's energy output if brought to scale. Develop scaled-up energy calculation considering power consumption. Explain energy source's environmental impact.
2	Photovoltaic Cell Investigation *design and results*	Group	Formative	Use Engineering Design Process. Design and implement investigation. Test, collect data, and chart light intensities and positions. Present results.
3	STEM Research Notebook *prompts*	Individual/ Group	Formative	Identify power output of an energy source and calculate the number of kilowatt-hours it produces.
3	STEM Research Notebook *prompts*	Individual	Formative	Explain how various renewable/ sustainable energy products for homes can be used in their own homes.
3	STEM Research Notebook *prompts*	Individual/ Group	Formative	Explain how power inverters in homes convert energy to volts.
3	Home Power System and Brochures *rubric*	Group	Summative	Identify power output of an energy source and calculate the number of kilowatt-hours it produces. Estimate number of hours an energy source can generate electricity based on environmental conditions (e.g., sunlight for solar, wind for windmills, etc.). Create a system of renewable/sustainable energy sources that can supply a minimum of 100% of a household's energy needs. Identify several ways to make a home more energy efficient (e.g., dual-pane windows, insulation, etc.). Explain importance of system to multiple demographic groups.

Continued

Table 3.5. (*Continued*)

Lesson	Assessment	Group/ Individual	Formative/ Summative	Lesson Objective Assessed
4	Innovation *rubric*	Group	Summative	Calculate the percentage of the world's energy demand a renewable/sustainable energy source covers. Make cogent arguments for the development of renewable/sustainable energy sources. Identify the ecological impact of a large-scale renewable/sustainable energy source. Identify the economic impact of a large-scale renewable/sustainable energy source.

MODULE TIMELINE

Tables 3.6–3.10 (pp. 39–42) provide lesson timelines for each week of the module. These timelines are provided for general guidance only and are based on class times of approximately 45 minutes.

Table 3.6. STEM Road Map Module Schedule Week One

Day 1	Day 2	Day 3	Day 4	Day 5
Lesson 1 *Generating Electricity* • Launch the module by discussing the use of fossil fuels for energy production, their pros and cons, and the need to find alternative sources of energy. • Explore the different forms of turbine power (steam versus motion energy) and analyze their processes.	*Lesson 1* Generating Electricity • Explore how turbines are used in conjunction with generators to produce electricity and analyze how electricity is transported to individual homes and businesses.	*Lesson 1* *Generating Electricity* • Students learn how to measure energy output in watts and the cost of energy to the consumer in kilowatt-hours. • Students explore how energy costs change in relation to the time of day (e.g., peak energy)	*Lesson 1* *Generating Electricity* • Students use galvanometers or multimeters to explore how the production of electricity varies with the speed by which a turbine moves.	*Lesson 1* *Generating Electricity* • Students build small watermills to connect to generators.

Table 3.7. STEM Road Map Module Schedule Week Two

Day 6	Day 7	Day 8	Day 9	Day 10
Lesson 1 *Generating Electricity* • Students connect their windmills or waterways to generators and measure their energy output as it relates to air or water speed.	*Lesson 1* *Generating Electricity* • Students present their findings on energy output of wind and water energy in a short essay • Students explain how the rate of change of the wind or water affects electrical output.	*Lesson 2* *Just the Tip of the Iceberg!* • Students are introduced to the history of solar energy and begin learning how photons are used to create electricity in photovoltaic cells.	*Lesson 2* *Just the Tip of the Iceberg!* • Students continue learning how solar panels work and are introduced to the next generation of solar energy.	*Lesson 2* *Just the Tip of the Iceberg!* • Students work in teams to search the Internet for as many alternative forms of renewable/sustainable energy sources as possible. Students then share their findings with the class.

Table 3.8. STEM Road Map Module Schedule Week Three

Day 11	Day 12	Day 13	Day 14	Day 15
Lesson 2 *Just the Tip of the Iceberg!* • Students select a renewable/sustainable energy source and begin researching how it works.	*Lesson 2* *Just the Tip of the Iceberg!* • Students research the costs of their energy sources and the impact they have on the environment.	*Lesson 2* *Just the Tip of the Iceberg!* • Students complete their individual research, write two-page essays, and prepare presentations of their energy source, outlining their costs, environmental impact, and feasibility.	*Lesson 2* *Just the Tip of the Iceberg!* • Student presentations on their energy sources.	*Lesson 2* *Just the Tip of the Iceberg!* • Student presentations on their energy sources.

Table 3.9. STEM Road Map Module Schedule Week Four

Day 16	Day 17	Day 18	Day 19	Day 20
Lesson 3 *Getting Off the Grid* • Students analyze the difference between watts and kilowatt-hours, learn to calculate kilowatt-hours from watts, and work in teams to estimate the number of kilowatt-hours average U.S. households use versus other countries and/or regions.	*Lesson 3* *Getting Off the Grid* • Students work in teams and search present-day, marketed technologies that use renewable/sustainable energies for home production of electricity (e.g., windmills, solar, hydrogen fuel cells, etc.). • Students begin creating their brochures.	*Lesson 3* *Getting Off the Grid* • Students design a home energy system using a combination of renewable/sustainable energy sources, which can power an average, single-family home. • Students calculate the energy output of each device used in their systems to determine if they can produce enough electricity to power a U.S. home.	*Lesson 3* *Getting Off the Grid* • Using systems of equations, students calculate the cost of their renewable/sustainable systems relative to an average power bill • Students complete their brochures.	*Lesson 4* *Powering the World* • Student teams brainstorm ideas for innovative, renewable/sustainable power sources and assign tasks for the presentation.

Table 3.10. STEM Road Map Module Schedule Week Five

Day 21	Day 22	Day 23	Day 24	Day 25
Lesson 4 *Powering the World* • Students create a design (drawing, computer-generated, model, etc.) of their product and work on their individual portions of the presentation.	*Lesson 4* *Powering the World* • Students discuss their individual work and give feedback to one another.	*Lesson 4* *Powering the World* • Team members pool their work and create a single, coherent presentation.	*Lesson 4* *Powering the World* • Teams present their challenge presentations.	*Lesson 4* *Powering the World* • Teams present their challenge presentations.

NATIONAL SCIENCE TEACHING ASSOCIATION

RESOURCES

Teachers have the option to co-teach portions of this module and may want to combine classes for activities such as developing timelines of energy development in the U.S. Computer science teachers can help students develop graphic images or animations, and art teachers can help students create three-dimensional models of turbines, electrical circuits, and students' innovative products. The media specialist can help teachers locate resources for students to view and read about electricity and energy production and issues surrounding the need to meet society's energy needs. Special educators and reading specialists can help find supplemental sources for students needing extra support in reading and writing. Additional resources may be found online. Community resources for this module may include guest speakers who work in energy production and electrical engineering, and those involved in resource conservation efforts related to energy.

REFERENCES

Keeley, P., and R. Harrington. 2010. *Uncovering student ideas in physical science, volume 1: 45 new force and motion assessment probes*. Arlington, VA: NSTA Press.

National Center for O*NET Development. *Find Occupations*. Retrieved from https://www.onetonline.org/find/

Peters-Burton, E. E., P. Seshaiyer, S. R. Burton, J. Drake-Patrick, and C. C. Johnson. 2015. The STEM Road Map for grades 9–12. In *STEM Road Map: A framework for integrated STEM education*, ed. C. C. Johnson, E. E. Peters-Burton, and T. J. Moore, 124–62. New York: Routledge. *www.routledge.com/products/9781138804234*.

WIDA Consortium. 2012. 2012 Amplification of the English language development standards: Kindergarten–grade 12. *www.wida.us/standards/eld.aspx*.

REBUILDING THE NATURAL ENVIRONMENT LESSON PLANS

Bradley Rankin, Anthony Pellegrino, Erin E. Peters-Burton,
Jennifer Drake Patrick, Janet B. Walton, and Carla C. Johnson

Lesson Plan 1: Generating Electricity

Since the ultimate goal of this module is for students to create an innovative and renewable/sustainable energy source, students need to know how we currently generate electricity. Learning about turbines and generators will encourage students to begin imagining new ways to move a turbine (rotating a turbine is not the only way to generate electricity, but it is one students should know). In this lesson, students will learn how energy sources such as hydroelectric, wind, or steam move turbines, how turbines are used to spin magnets within a series of wires, and how the electrons in the wires begin to move in a specific direction creating electrical current. Students will build small models of watermills or waterways (simulating water moving through a dam) to move a turbine connected to a generator. Students will explore how the rate of the wind or water flow affects the turbine and electrical generation. Students will begin generating ideas for their companies' renewable energy sources. Students will also begin to gain an awareness of the impact electricity has had on society for the last 130 years, how it has spurred the oil economy, impacted the ecosystem, and changed reality for various groups of people.

ESSENTIAL QUESTIONS

- What is electricity?

- What is a volt, an ampere, and an ohm?

- How is electricity generated, transported, and used in everyday life?

- What have been the impacts of electricity on society?

DOI: 10.4324/9781003261711-7

ESTABLISHED GOALS AND OBJECTIVES

At the conclusion of this lesson, students will be able to do the following:

- Understand that a force, in the form of voltage, can moves electrons in elements such as copper in a specific direction

- Understand that resistors slow electrical current (measured in ohms), and work in conjunction with voltage and current to create circuits that allow devices to receive the electricity that makes them work

- Understand the basics of the electro-magnetic force; understand that a magnetic field affects the movement of electrons.

- Understand how electricity is generated and transported

- Do basic calculations involving volts and amperes

TIME REQUIRED

- 7 days (approximately 45 minutes each day; see Tables 3.6–3.7, pp. 39–40)

MATERIALS

Required Materials for Lesson 1

- STEM Research Notebooks (1 per student)

- Computer or device with internet connection (1 per student)

Additional Materials for Linear or Steam Motion Energy Source Activity (1 per team of 3–4 students)

- Generator such as this one from Flinn Scientific https://www.flinnsci.com/electric-generator/ap6043/

  - OR solenoid (such as this one from Flinn Scientific https://www.flinnsci.com/air-core-solenoid/ap5628/)
  - and strong permanent magnets such as neodymium

- galvanometers or bench meters that measure 0–5 Volts

- Circuit Construction Kit or assorted batteries, light bulbs, wire, and wire cutters

- Materials for building small watermills and waterways (e.g., balsa wood, straws, fans, etc.).

SAFETY NOTES

1. All students must wear safety glasses or goggles during all phases of this inquiry activity.

2. Use caution when working with sharps (screw eye hooks, toothpicks, etc.) to avoid cutting or puncturing skin.

3. Make sure all materials are put away after completing the activity.

4. Wash hands with soap and water after completing this activity.

CONTENT STANDARDS AND KEY VOCABULARY

Table 4.1 lists the content standards from the *Next Generation Science Standards (NGSS)*, *Common Core State Standards*, and the Framework for 21st Century Learning that this lesson addresses, and Table 4.2 presents the key vocabulary. Vocabulary terms are provided for both teacher and student use. Teachers may choose to introduce some or all of the terms to students.

Table 4.1. Content Standards Addressed in STEM Road Map Module Lesson 1

NEXT GENERATION SCIENCE STANDARDS

PERFORMANCE EXPECTATIONS

• HS-PS3–3. Design, build, and refine a device that works within given constraints to convert one form of energy into another form of energy.

DISCIPLINARY CORE IDEAS
PS3.A. Definitions of Energy

• At the macroscopic scale, energy manifests itself in multiple ways, such as in motion, sound, light, and thermal energy.

PS3.D. Energy in Chemical Processes

• Although energy cannot be destroyed, it can be converted to less useful forms – for example, to thermal energy in the surrounding environment.

ETS1.A. Defining and Delimiting an Engineering Problem

• Criteria and constraints also include satisfying any requirements set by society, such as taking issues of risk mitigation into account, and they should be quantified to the extent possible and stated in such a way that one can tell if a given design meets them. (secondary)

Continued

Table 4.1. (*continued*)

CROSSCUTTING CONCEPTS

Energy and Matter

- Changes of energy and matter in a system can be described in terms of energy and matter flows into, out of, and within that system.

Connections to Engineering, Technology, and Applications of Science

- Influence of science, engineering and technology on society and the natural world
- Modern civilization depends on major technological systems. Engineers continuously modify these technological systems by applying scientific knowledge and engineering design practices to increase benefits while decreasing costs and risks.

SCIENCE AND ENGINEERING PRACTICES

Constructing Explanations and Designing Solutions

- Constructing explanations and designing solutions in 9–12 builds on K–8 experiences and progresses to explanations and designs that are supported by multiple and independent student-generated sources of evidence consistent with scientific ideas, principles, and theories.
- Design, evaluate, and/or refine a solution to a complex real-world problem, based on scientific knowledge, student-generated sources of evidence, prioritized criteria, and tradeoff considerations

COMMON CORE STATE STANDARDS FOR MATHEMATICS

MATHEMATICAL PRACTICES

- MP1. Make sense of problems and persevere in solving them.
- MP3. Construct viable arguments and critique the reasoning of others.
- MP5. Use appropriate tools strategically.
- MP6. Attend to precision.
- MP7. Look for and make use of structure.
- MP8. Look for and express regularity in repeated reasoning.

COMMON CORE STATE STANDARDS FOR ENGLISH LANGUAGE ARTS

READING STANDARDS

- RI.9–10.1. Cite strong and thorough textual evidence to support analysis of what the text says explicitly as well as inferences drawn from the text. a. Develop factual, interpretive, and evaluative questions for further exploration of the topic(s).
- RI.9–10.2. Determine a central idea of a text and analyze its development over the course of the text, including how it emerges and is shaped and refined by specific details; provide an objective summary of the text.

- RI.9–10.3. Analyze how the author unfolds an analysis or series of ideas or events, including the order in which the points are made, how they are introduced and developed, and the connections that are drawn between them.
- RI.9–10.4. Determine the meaning of words and phrases as they are used in a text, including figurative, connotative, and technical meanings; analyze the cumulative impact of specific word choices on meaning and tone (e.g., how the language of a court opinion differs from that of a newspaper).

SPEAKING AND LISTENING STANDARDS

- SL.9–10.1a-d. Engage effectively in a range of collaborative discussions (one-on-one, in groups, and teacher-led) with diverse partners on *grade 10 topics, texts, and issues*, building on others' ideas and expressing their own clearly.

   a. Come to discussions prepared, having read or studied required material; explicitly draw on that preparation by referring to evidence on the topic, text, or issue to probe and reflect on ideas under discussion.
   b. Follow rules for collegial discussions, set specific goals and deadlines, and define individual roles as needed.
   c. Pose and respond to specific questions with elaboration and detail by making comments that contribute to the topic, text, or issue under discussion.
   d. Review the key ideas expressed and demonstrate understanding of multiple perspectives through reflection and paraphrasing.
   e. Seek to understand and communicate with individuals from different perspectives and cultural backgrounds.

- SL.9–10.2. Interpret information presented in diverse media and formats (e.g., visually, quantitatively, orally) and explain how it contributes to a topic, text, or issue under study.
- SL.9–10.4. Present claims and findings, sequencing ideas logically and using pertinent descriptions, facts, and details to accentuate main ideas or themes; use appropriate eye contact, adequate volume, and clear pronunciation.

FRAMEWORK FOR 21ST CENTURY LEARNING
Information Literacy; Media Literacy; ICT Literacy; Flexibility and Adaptability; Initiative and Self-Direction; Social and Cross Cultural Skills; Productivity and Accountability; Leadership and Responsibility

Table 4.2. Key Vocabulary in Lesson One

Key Vocabulary	Definition
ampere or amp	the International System of Units (SI) unit for electric current; named after André-Marie Ampère (1775–1836), French mathematician and physicist; .
electron	a subatomic particle, symbol e– or β –, with a negative elementary electric charge

Continued

Table 4.2. (*continued*)

Key Vocabulary	Definition
energy source	sources from which energy can be obtained to provide heat, light, and power; include human and animal power, fossil fuels, uranium, water power, wind, and the Sun.
generator	any device for converting mechanical energy into electrical energy by electromagnetic induction, especially a large one as in a power station
steam turbine	a machine for producing power that uses the thermal energy from pressurized steam to turn a rotating shaft connected to a generator; invented by Sir Charles Parsons in 1884
transformer	an electrical device that transfers electrical energy between two or more circuits through electromagnetic induction; commonly used to increase or decrease the voltages of alternating current in electric power applications.
turbine	a rotary mechanical device that extracts energy from a fluid flow and converts it into useful work; a machine with at least one moving part called a rotor assembly, which is a shaft or drum with blades attached
volt	the difference in electric potential between two points of a conducting wire when an electric current of one ampere dissipates one watt of power between those points
water turbine	a rotary engine that converts kinetic and potential energy of water into mechanical work
watt	the SI unit of power used to measure the rate of energy transfer.
wind turbine	a turbine having large vanes and a wheel rotated by the wind to generate electricity.

TEACHER BACKGROUND INFORMATION

In this module, students have the opportunity to form a coherent, worldview of energy production and consumption. In order to address the module challenge, students must not only know how energy is produced, but also how it is an integral part of the world's economy, how it affects the world's ecosystem, and how it shapes humans' worldviews. Students must understand the social, economic, and environmental ramifications of energy production and consumption in order to create economic and environmental impact reports. Students will also need to understand how energy consumption and production is interpreted differently by various groups of people (e.g., liberals versus conservatives) in order to create advertisements designed to appeal to various groups. Links to websites that cover the core topics in this module are provided below.

- For information about the history and science of fossil fuels, see:
  - *www.thirteen.org/wnet/extremeoil/history/*
  - *www.pbs.org/wnet/extremeoil/history/*
  - *www.pbslearningmedia.org/search/?q=oil&selected_facets=*

- For information about electricity and how it is generated, see:
  - *www.youtube.com/watch?v=mUMAfSBR4yg*
  - *www.youtube.com/watch?v=bGb2lJdJJRE*
  - *www.youtube.com/results?search_query=how+electricity+is+generated*

- For information about renewable and nonrenewable energy sources, see:
  - *www.eia.gov/energyexplained/index.php*
  - *Jeremy Rifkin's (2003) book, The Hydrogen Economy*

For examples of energy innovations, see:

- *www.youtube.com/watch?v=bvlolmFX-rc*
- *https://www.greenmatters.com/news/2017/10/20/1hIiS2/high-altitude-wind-farms-game-changer*
- *www.youtube.com/watch?v=uStFvcz9Or4*
- *www.youtube.com/watch?v=shkFDPI6kGE*

COMMON MISCONCEPTIONS

Students will have various types of prior knowledge about the concepts introduced in this lesson. Table 4.3 outlines some common misconceptions students may have concerning these concepts. Because of the breadth of students' experiences, it is not possible to anticipate every misconception that students may bring as they approach this lesson. Incorrect or inaccurate prior understanding of concepts can influence student learning in the future, however, so it is important to be alert to misconceptions such as those presented in the table.

Table 4.3. Common Misconceptions About the Concepts in Lesson 1

Topic	Student Misconception	Explanation
Electricity	Electric current adds electrons to empty wires or other conductors.	The substances that act as conductors have free electrons in them that are already moving, but at a very slow pace and not all in one direction. A battery or generator can create an electric current in the substance by pushing the electrons through it.
	Electricity is a primary source of energy.	Electricity is actually an energy carrier (sometimes called a secondary source). Electricity must be produced by a primary energy source like coal, natural gas, nuclear energy, or wind.
Innovations in energy	While energy-efficiency undoubtedly has long-term value, adding a bunch of energy-efficient features to a new home will drive its cost up significantly	As energy-efficiency has gotten more popular, research and development has made it more affordable

PREPARATION FOR LESSON 1

Review the Teacher Background Information (p. 25), assemble the materials for the lesson, and preview the recommended videos and websites. Prepare checklists or rubrics for the key points that should be elicited by students when you ask them the questions in this lesson. You also may want to prepare a roster of students for each class so that you can record each student's level of participation in the class discussions as a formative assessment. Have your students set up their STEM Research Notebooks (see pp. 26–28 for discussion and student instruction handout). Students should include all work for the module in the STEM Research Notebook, so you may wish to have them include section dividers in their notebooks.

Assemble 2 or 3 pictures of high altitude wind turbines. Ensure students have access to the Internet, and make sure you have enough generators and galvanometers (or multimeters) for teams of students to explore how electricity is generated and to test their energy sources.

LEARNING PLAN COMPONENTS
Introductory Activity/Engagement

Connection to the Challenge: Begin each day of this lesson by directing students' attention to the driving question for the module, "How can electricity be generated in a renewable/sustainable way for use in everyday life?" Continue by asking "How is electricity generated, transported, and used in everyday life? What have been the impacts of electricity on society?" Introduce students to the module challenge on the first day, and remind students of the challenge at the start of each class:

> *You and your fellow team members have decided to start a company that will change the way the world uses energy. Your primary goal is to create an innovative power source that is both sustainable and renewable. It can be something entirely new, a spinoff from a present technology, or a creative mixture of several technologies. In order to be a profitable company, the cost-benefit ratio of creating your innovative energy source must be considered, as must your ability to market the innovation to as many people as possible. Furthermore, your team must consider all the ways your innovation will impact the environment and the world's economy. Your team must also convince investors, politicians, and everyday people that your innovation is worthwhile.*

On the first day of the module, hand out the Energy Innovation Challenge student handout to each student (see p. 61).

Hold a brief student discussion of how their learning in the previous days' lesson(s) contributed to their ability to create their innovation for the final challenge. You may wish to hold a class discussion, creating a class list of key ideas on chart paper or the board, or you may wish to have students create a STEM Research Notebook entry with this information.

Science Class: To activate prior student knowledge and initiate discussion about energy sources, show students images of high-altitude wind turbines and have students share their ideas about what they are and their experiences with seeing these types of turbines. Next, show students a video clip about high altitude wind turbines such as *www.youtube.com/watch?v=kldA4nWANA8*. Hold a class discussion about wind turbines as an alternative to fossil fuels for energy production, eliciting responses and/or opinions from students about why countries all over the world are pursuing technologies such as high-altitude wind turbines. Have students share their ideas about the advantages and the disadvantages of using fossil fuels such as coal to produce energy. Focus students' attention on the non-renewability of fossil fuels and prompt discussion about alternative energy sources. Tell students that in this module they will be challenged to work in teams to create energy companies that create and market innovative ways to create energy.

Have students discuss their understanding of electricity generation, using the questions provided in the STEM Research Notebook prompt, within teams of 3–4 students each and record their ideas in their STEM Research Notebooks. Then, have students share their ideas with the class.

STEM Research Notebook Prompt

Ask students to respond to the following questions: (a) What is electricity? (b) How is it generated? (c) How does it get to our houses?

Mathematics Connection: Ask students to estimate how much electricity is needed to power a refrigerator, a television, and a home water heater and whether they think each needs different amounts of electricity. Ask students why or why not they think these devices need different amounts of electricity. Have students look up energy usage for these household appliances and record their findings in their STEM Research Notebooks. The following website is an example of resources that students can use: *www.siliconvalleypower.com/for-residents/save-energy/appliance-energy-use-chart.*

ELA Connection: Have students work in teams to discuss how people's lives were different prior to widespread access to electricity in homes. Have students record their ideas in their STEM Research Notebooks. Next, have students should research historical accounts from the time before electrical power. For example:

- "History of Electricity" by the Institute for Energy Research at *www.instituteforenergyresearch.org/history-electricity/*

- "Rural Life was Very Hard Before Electricity" at *www.paynesvillearea.com/news/turnofcentury/turnofcentury030800.htm*

- "Life Before and After Electricity" by an 8th grade student at *www.youtube.com/watch?v=8HbzaOv8HZ0*

- "Electricity's impact on Rural Life" at *www.ncpedia.org/agriculture/electricity*

Social Studies Connection: Have students work in teams to discuss their ideas about when electrical power was first used how it was first generated. Have students record their ideas in their STEM Research Notebooks.

Activity/Exploration

Science Class: Students will be challenged to create a linear or steam motion energy source used with a turbine that works in conjunction with a generator.

Linear or Steam Motion Energy Source Activity

Using generators, (or solenoids and neodymium magnets), a circuit construction kit, and materials for building small watermills and waterways (e.g., balsa wood, straws, fans, etc.), student groups will construct a small watermill that will move the generator to create electrical energy from mechanical energy that is provided by the waterway. Students will using the engineering design process to research how waterwheels are constructed and draw a plan in the STEM Research Notebook. Student teams will then request the materials to build their prototype waterwheel or waterway and build their prototype. Students will test the amount of mechanical energy versus (input) versus the amount of electrical energy they produce and record these variables in their STEM Research Notebook. The amount of electricity generated will be measured by the galvanometer, which will be wired into the circuit connecting the watermill and the generator (see diagram below). Student groups will be challenged to vary the speed by which they move their turbines at least six times and list the electrical outputs in order to make a generalization of the rate of mechanical motion to electrical generation. Students must write a one-to-two-page paper describing their device, the process by which they generated electricity, and what they found when altering the rate of mechanical motion. A rubric is provided at the end of the lesson to assess student work.

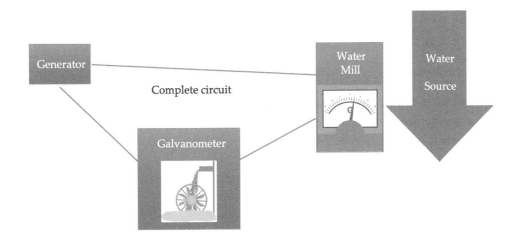

Mathematics Connection: Students will study Ohm's law and learn how the relationship between voltage, amperes, and ohms work in conjunction with one another to create circuits. Using an online simulation such as https://phet.colorado.edu/en/simulation/circuit-construction-kit-dc, have students manipulate voltage (V), amps (I), and ohms (R) and record the values in their STEM Research Notebooks. From the data table, students should examine the patterns that they find to understand the relationship of these variables. Finally, students should create an argument using a claim, for example the relationship of voltage, amperage and resistance can be expressed in the formula $V = IR$, backed by evidence that they derive from their data tables. Next, have students plan an investigation to determine the relationship between voltage, amperes, and ohms using a circuit kit. Students should record their information in their STEM Research Notebook as indicated below.

STEM Research Notebook Prompt

Create an investigation to determine the relationship between voltage, amperes. Record your research question(s), procedures, and data tables in your STEM Research

Notebook. Check your plan with your teacher before gathering data by manipulating the simulation elements.

Once your design is approved, collect data and make a claim about the relationship between voltage, amperes, and ohms. Defend your claim with evidence from the simulation.

ELA Connection: Students will research how electricity changed the lives of various groups of people (e.g., households http://xroads.virginia.edu/~drbr/r_uth.html, farmers, manufacturers, etc.). Have students create Powerpoint presentations to describe the impacts on a particular segment of the population.

Some useful websites include the following:

- *www.xroads.virginia.edu/~drbr/r_uth.html*

- *www.reference.com/history/did-electricity-impact-society-3d108662bc468b61*

- *www.americanhistory.si.edu/lighting/19thcent/consq19.htm*

Social Studies Connection: Students will investigate the means by which electricity was originally generated and begin researching the advent of an oil economy. A helpful website is the PBS site on Extreme Oil - http://www.pbs.org/wnet/extremeoil/history/

Students should work in teams of 3–4 to create a timeline from one of the following time segments:

- Pre-history – 1849

- 1850–1929

- 1930–1974

- 1975-Present

Teams will then present their timelines and explain the "era" for each of the time segments.

Explanation

Science Class: Demonstrate to the class how the rate at which magnets move through a coil of wires affects electricity while students observe and take notes of the demonstration in their STEM Research Notebooks. To do the demonstration, set up a solenoid and show students a neodymium magnet. Connect the solenoid to a galvanometer to measure electricity flowing through a wire. Slowly move the magnet in and out of the solenoid and have students note the amount of electricity on the galvanometer (small amount). Next quickly move the magnet in and out of the solenoid and have the students note the amount of electricity on the galvanometer (large amount). Next show a video of a generator such as the "Electricity Generator Demonstration" at *www.youtube.com/watch?v=MxNQ6sOLgSs* and have students respond to the STEM Research Notebook prompt below.

STEM Research Notebook Prompt

As you watch the generator demonstration, record the different variables that can change the amount of electricity that is generated. After watching the video, discuss with your team what you recorded. Determine one variable that your group would like to test, such as the effect of the number of coils on the amount of electricity generated, and compose a research question for your study. Design and record your procedure and data table. Check your design with your teacher before gathering data. Be sure that you have answered your research question.

Have students review the concepts of energy sources, turbines, generators, transformers, power stations, and electricity transport to solidify student understanding of the entire system. Students should perform this review by completing the Review of Major Concepts graphic organizer found at the end of the lesson from the materials they have recorded in their STEM Research Notebooks.

Mathematics Connection: Guide students in manipulating the formula $V = IR$ to determine the amount of one variable needed given the other two.

ELA Connection: Pool students' research and foster whole-class discussions on the social ramification of near-ubiquitous electricity. Extend this discussion to how actual world-wide ubiquity of electricity can affect all humans in all walks of life. Have students write a one-page, first-person, narrative describing daily routines from the perspective of an adolescent who lives without consistent access to electricity, and then write a similar narrative from the perspective of an adolescent who has constant access to electricity.

Social Studies Connection: Have students continue to present their timelines. Guide discussions on how widespread access to electricity was brought about the oil economy, and begin developing an overall class-generated timeline for the exponential growth of the oil industry.

Elaboration/Application of Knowledge

Science Class: Have students sketch a prototype for a steam turbine based upon what they found out about the mechanisms of a windmill and waterway. Have students respond to the STEM Research Notebook prompt below.

STEM Research Notebook Prompt

Compare and contrast the way electricity is produced by a windmill, a waterway, and a steam turbine. Answer the following questions:

- What is similar across all of those technologies? What is different about each technology?

- How is the mechanical energy created to make each a windmill, waterway and a steam turbine move?

- Which ones are renewable resources?

- Which ones create the most electricity?

- What are the limitations of each technology? The benefits of each?

Each student team should discuss their answers with another student team to form a consensus.

Mathematics Connection: Have students conduct internet research to determine what voltage is needed to move electricity from a power plant to a neighborhood transformer and why such a large voltage is needed, and record their findings in the STEM Research Notebook prompt below.

STEM Research Notebook Prompt

Conduct internet research to determine what voltage is needed to move electricity from a power plant to a neighborhood transformer and why such a large voltage is needed. Answer the following questions:

- What is the voltage needed by large appliances such as a refrigerator versus small appliances such as a coffee maker?

- What current is needed? What is the relationship between voltage and current?

- Why are there differences in the amounts of voltage and amperage countries use in households?

ELA Connection: Have students write a short story about a world that loses power entirely, emphasizing how different groups of people would fare in such a place.

Social Studies Connection: Have students write a paper on the alternative history that could have occurred if Thomas Edison and Nikola Tesla had to use wind energy because there was no knowledge of fossil fuels.

Evaluation/Assessment

Students may be assessed on the following performance tasks and other measures listed.

Performance Tasks

- Voltage, Amperage, and Ohms Investigation Designs and Results

- Electric Generator Investigation Design and Results

- Review of Major Concepts Graphic Organizer

- Windmill, Waterway or Steam Turbine Prototype and Paper

Other Measures

- STEM Research Notebook Prompts

- Participation in class discussions

INTERNET RESOURCES

History and science of fossil fuels

- *www.thirteen.org/wnet/extremeoil/history/*

- *www.pbs.org/wnet/extremeoil/history/*

- *www.pbslearningmedia.org/search/?q=oil&selected_facets=*

Electricity and how it is generated

- *www.youtube.com/watch?v=mUMAfSBR4yg*

- *www.youtube.com/watch?v=bGb2lJdJJRE*

- *www.youtube.com/results?search_query=how+electricity+is+generated*

Renewable and nonrenewable energy sources

- *www.eia.gov/energyexplained/index.php*

Examples of energy innovations

- *www.youtube.com/watch?v=bvlolmFX-rc*

- *https://www.greenmatters.com/news/2017/10/20/1hIiS2/high-altitude-wind-farms-game-changer*

- *www.youtube.com/watch?v=uStFvcz9Or4*

- *www.youtube.com/watch?v=shkFDPI6kGE*

high altitude wind turbines

- *www.youtube.com/watch?v=kldA4nWANA8*

Appliance energy usage

- *www.siliconvalleypower.com/for-residents/save-energy/appliance-energy-use-chart.*

History of Electricity

- *www.instituteforenergyresearch.org/history-electricity/*

Impact of electricity on people's lives

- *www.paynesvillearea.com/news/turnofcentury/turnofcentury030800.htm*

- *www.youtube.com/watch?v=8HbzaOv8HZ0*

- *www.ncpedia.org/agriculture/electricity*

Circuit simulation

- *https://phet.colorado.edu/en/simulation/circuit-construction-kit-dc*

Impact of electricity on various demographic groups

- *www.xroads.virginia.edu/~drbr/r_uth.html*

- *www.reference.com/history/did-electricity-impact-society-3d108662bc468b61*

- *www.americanhistory.si.edu/lighting/19thcent/consq19.htm*

PBS, Extreme Oil

- *http://www.pbs.org/wnet/extremeoil/history/*

Generator demonstration

- *www.youtube.com/watch?v=MxNQ6sOLgSs*

ENERGY INNOVATION CHALLENGE

STUDENT HANDOUT

You and your fellow team members have decided to start a company that will change the way the world uses energy. Your primary goal is to create an innovative power source that is both sustainable and renewable. It can be something entirely new, a spinoff from a present technology, or a creative mixture of several technologies. In order to be a profitable company, the cost-benefit ratio of creating your innovative energy source must be considered, as must your ability to market the innovation to as many people as possible. Furthermore, your team must consider all the ways your innovation will impact the environment and the world's economy. In order to convince investors, politicians, and everyday people that your innovation is worthwhile, your team must do the following:

1. Identify your innovation

2. Create a diagram (drawn, computer-generated, etc.)

3. Thoroughly describe how the innovation works

4. Create a cost-benefit ratio of creating your innovative energy source

5. Determine the approach to market the innovation to as many people as possible

6. Create a cost-benefit ratio of creating your innovative energy source

7. Determine the approach to market the innovation to as many people as possible

8. Determine a conservative amount of kilowatt-hours an individual unit produces per day

   a. Use your knowledge of other energy sources (wind, hydro-electric, solar, etc.) to determine your amount

9. Estimate the amount of fossil fuels that will not be used when your innovation is scaled up to the entire country or world

   a. Your estimate must be supported by realistic data and the appropriate mathematics must be shown to justify your estimate.

Additionally, your team must divide up the following jobs:

1. One person must write an environmental report on your innovation and state all of the positive and negative impacts it may have.

2. One person must write a report on the impact your innovation will have on the world's economy when the use of fossil fuels is decreased due to your innovation.

3. One person must market the innovation to at least four distinct demographic groups (e.g., conservationists, conservatives, liberals, etc.) by creating advertisements tailored to each group.

4. One person must pool the information gathered by your team and the individual members who wrote the environmental and economic impact reports and create a presentation to give to the class.

5. One person must fact-check all of the work done by the group as a whole and as individuals. S/he must edit the impact reports, advertisements, and presentation and make sure all sources are referenced.

Review of Major Concepts

Concept	Define the concept. How is it used?
Energy Sources	
Turbines	
Generators	
Transformers	
Power Stations	
Electricity transport	

Linear or Steam Motion Energy Source Rubric

	Expert (4)	Competent (3)	Emerging (2)	Did not meet expectations (1)	Score
Energy Source/ Turbine Comments	The source used linear or steam motion properly with a turbine such that electricity was generated when connected to a generator	The source used linear or steam motion properly with a turbine such that electricity was generated when connected to a generator but it was slightly inefficient due to minor flaws in the design	The source used linear or steam motion decently with a turbine such that electricity was generated when connected to a generator but it was fairly inefficient due to significant flaws in the design	The design was haphazard and fell apart easily, making its potential to generate electricity inconsistent due to frequent breakdown of the energy source	
Data Collection Comments	Data collection included at least six measurements that accurately showed that the electricity generation was proportional to the rate of change of the wind, water, or steam	Data collection included at least six measurements that mostly showed that the electricity generation was proportional to the rate of change of the wind, water, or steam	Data collection included five or less measurements that accurately showed that the electricity generation was proportional to the rate of change of the wind, water, or steam	There were four or less data points and the data were inaccurate.	
Thoroughness of Paper Comments	The paper described the entire process of creating the energy source, how it was used to generate electricity, the electromagnetic process that governs electricity generation, and a description about the rate at which the wind, water, or steam proportionally affected the electricity generation	The paper described each of the criteria in the previous column with a few mistakes	The paper left out one of the criterion described in the first column and those that were described have a few mistakes	The paper left out two or more of the criteria described in the first column, and the remaining criteria have several mistakes	
Grammatical Quality of Paper Comments	The paper is clear and concise. There are no grammatical mistakes	The paper is clear and concise with few grammatical mistakes	The paper is decently clear with several mistakes	The paper is difficult to read, makes little mistakes, and has several grammatical mistakes	
Total Score					

Lesson Plan 2: Just the Tip of the Iceberg!

In this lesson, students will learn that fossil fuels, wind, and hydroelectric power are not the only ways to rotate turbines. Furthermore, students will learn that the turbines/generator model is not the only way to create energy in a renewable and sustainable manner and will explore photovoltaic cells as a way to harness the Sun's energy for human use. Students will explore several other methods – past, present, and futuristic – to generate electricity.

ESSENTIAL QUESTIONS

- What are several ways electricity can be produced without fossil fuels?

- What are the differences between renewable and sustainable energy sources?

- What are examples of renewable and sustainable energy sources?

- How is solar power generated in photovoltaic cells, and how is this different than wind or hydroelectric energy?

ESTABLISHED GOALS AND OBJECTIVES

At the conclusion of this lesson, students will be able to do the following:

- Understand and be able to identify several first, second, third, and future generations of renewable/sustainable energy sources.

- Understand how energy is generated using photovoltaic cells.

- Analyze how forms of renewable energy work, their potential energy output if brought to scale, and their environmental impact.

TIME REQUIRED

8 days (approximately 45 minutes per day; see Tables 3.7–3.8, p. 40)

MATERIALS

Required Materials for Lesson 2 (1 per student)

- Computers with Internet access

- Small photovoltaic cells

- Galvanometers

SAFETY NOTES

1. All students must wear safety glasses or goggles during all phases of this inquiry activity.

2. Keep electrical wires away from water sources because of the shock hazard.

3. Use only GFI protected electrical receptacles.

4. Wash hands with soap and water after completing this activity.

CONTENT STANDARDS AND KEY VOCABULARY

Table 4.4 lists the content standards from the *Next Generation Science Standards (NGSS),* *Common Core State Standards,* and the Framework for 21st Century Learning that this lesson addresses, and Table 4.5 presents the key vocabulary. Vocabulary terms are provided for both teacher and student use. Teachers may choose to introduce some or all of the terms to students

Table 4.4. Standards Addressed in STEM Road Map Module Lesson 2

<table>
<tr><td>

NEXT GENERATION SCIENCE STANDARDS

PERFORMANCE EXPECTATIONS

- HS-ETS1–3. Evaluate a solution to a complex real-world problem based on prioritized criteria and trade-offs that account for a range of constraints, including cost, safety, reliability, and aesthetics as well as possible social, cultural, and environmental impacts.

DISCIPLINARY CORE IDEAS
ETS1.B. Developing Possible Solutions

- When evaluating solutions, it is important to take into account a range of constraints, including cost, safety, reliability, and aesthetics, and to consider social, cultural, and environmental impacts.

CROSSCUTTING CONCEPTS

Systems and System Models

- Models (e.g., physical, mathematical, computer models) can be used to simulate systems and interactions – including energy, matter, and information flows – within and between systems at different scales.

Connections to Engineering, Technology, and Applications of Science

- Influence of science, engineering and technology on society and the natural world
</td></tr>
</table>

- New technologies can have deep impacts on society and the environment, including some that were not anticipated. Analysis of costs and benefits is a critical aspect of decisions about technology.

MATHEMATICAL PRACTICES

- MP1. Make sense of problems and persevere in solving them.
- MP3. Construct viable arguments and critique the reasoning of others.
- MP5. Use appropriate tools strategically.
- MP6. Attend to precision.
- MP7. Look for and make use of structure.
- MP8. Look for and express regularity in repeated reasoning.

COMMON CORE STATE STANDARDS FOR ENGLISH LANGUAGE ARTS

READING STANDARDS

- RI.9–10.1. Cite strong and thorough textual evidence to support analysis of what the text says explicitly as well as inferences drawn from the text. a. Develop factual, interpretive, and evaluative questions for further exploration of the topic(s).
- RI.9–10.2. Determine a central idea of a text and analyze its development over the course of the text, including how it emerges and is shaped and refined by specific details; provide an objective summary of the text.
- RI.9–10.3. Analyze how the author unfolds an analysis or series of ideas or events, including the order in which the points are made, how they are introduced and developed, and the connections that are drawn between them.
- RI.9–10.4. Determine the meaning of words and phrases as they are used in a text, including figurative, connotative, and technical meanings; analyze the cumulative impact of specific word choices on meaning and tone (e.g., how the language of a court opinion differs from that of a newspaper).

WRITING STANDARDS

- W.9–10.1a-e Write arguments to support claims in an analysis of substantive topics or texts, using valid reasoning and relevant and sufficient evidence. Explore and inquire into areas of interest to formulate an argument.

  a) Introduce precise claim(s), distinguish the claim(s) from alternate or opposing claims, and create an organization that establishes clear relationships among claim(s), counterclaims, reasons, and evidence.
  b) Develop claim(s) and counterclaims fairly, supplying evidence for each while pointing out the strengths and limitations of both in a manner that anticipates the audience's knowledge level and concerns.
  c) Use words, phrases, and clauses to link the major sections of the text, create cohesion, and clarify the relationships between claim(s) and reasons, between reasons and evidence, and between claim(s) and counterclaims.

Continued

Table 4.4. (*continued*)

---

d) Establish and maintain a formal style and objective tone while attending to the norms and conventions of the discipline in which they are writing.

e) Provide a concluding statement or section that follows from and supports the argument presented.

- W.9–10.2a-f Write informative/explanatory texts to examine and convey complex ideas, concepts, and information clearly and accurately through the effective selection, organization, and analysis of content.

  a) Introduce a topic; organize complex ideas, concepts, and information to make important connections and distinctions; include formatting (e.g., headings), graphics (e.g., figures, tables), and multimedia when useful to aiding comprehension.

  b) Develop the topic with well-chosen, relevant, and sufficient facts, extended definitions, concrete details, quotations, or other information and examples appropriate to the audience's knowledge of the topic.

  c) Use appropriate and varied transitions to link the major sections of the text, create cohesion, and clarify the relationships among complex ideas and concepts.

  d) Use precise language and domain-specific vocabulary to manage the complexity of the topic.

  e) Establish and maintain a formal style and objective tone while attending to the norms and conventions of the discipline in which they are writing.

  f) Provide a concluding statement or section that follows from and supports the information or explanation presented (e.g., articulating implications or the significance of the topic).

- W.9–10.4 Produce clear and coherent writing in which the development, organization, and style are appropriate to task, purpose, and audience.
- W.9–10.5. Develop and strengthen writing as needed by planning, revising, editing, rewriting, or trying a new approach, focusing on addressing what is most significant for a specific purpose and audience.
- W.9–10.7. Conduct short as well as more sustained research projects to answer a question (including a self-generated question) or solve a problem; narrow or broaden the inquiry when appropriate; synthesize multiple sources on the subject, demonstrating understanding of the subject under investigation.
- W.9–10.8. Gather relevant information from multiple authoritative print and digital sources, using advanced searches effectively; assess the usefulness of each source in answering the research question; integrate information into the text selectively to maintain the flow of ideas, avoiding plagiarism and following a standard format for citation.
- W.9–10.9a-b. Draw evidence from literary or informational texts to support analysis, reflection, and research.
- Apply *grades 9–10 Reading standards* to literature (e.g., "Analyze how an author draws on and transforms source material in a specific work
- Apply *grades 9–10 Reading standards* to literary nonfiction (e.g., "Delineate and evaluate the argument and specific claims in a text, assessing whether the reasoning is valid and the evidence is relevant and sufficient; identify false statements and fallacious reasoning").

Table 4.5. Key Vocabulary in Lesson Two

Key Vocabulary	Definition
1st generation technologies	energy technologies that emerged from the industrial revolution at the end of the 19th century and include hydropower, biomass combustion and geothermal power and heat
2nd generation technologies	energy technologies that resulted from investments prompted by energy security concerns linked to the U.S. oil crises in 1973 and 1979; include solar heating and cooling, wind power, modern forms of bioenergy and solar photovoltaics
3rd generation technologies	energy technologies that are currently under development; include advanced biomass gasification, bio refinery technologies, concentrating solar thermal power, hot dry rock geothermal energy and ocean energy.

Continued

Table 4.5. *(continued)*

Key Vocabulary	Definition
carbon-negative	describes a process that results in the permanent removal of carbon dioxide from Earth's atmosphere; considered the direct opposite of carbon dioxide emission
carbon-neutral	describes a situation of net zero carbon emissions achieved by balancing carbon release with equivalent amounts of carbon sequestration or offset; used in the context of carbon dioxide releasing processes associated with transportation, energy production, and industrial processes
kilowatt-hour (kwh)	An electrical energy measurement equal to 1000 watts per hour.
nonrenewable resource	a natural resource that cannot replenish itself quickly enough to outpace usage and consumption
photovoltaic cell	a panel that allows solar energy to be converted into direct current electricity
renewable resource	a natural resource that can replenish itself quickly enough to outpace usage and consumption, either through biological reproduction or other naturally recurring processes
sustainable resource	a resource that can be maintained at a steady level without exhausting natural resources or causing severe ecological damage

TEACHER BACKGROUND INFORMATION

Renewable/Sustainable Energy Sources

In this lesson, students will expand their understanding of electricity generation to include types of renewable and sustainable energy sources. This will spur imaginations for coming up with an electricity innovation. For instance, students who learn about wearable kinetic devices that create enough electricity to power their phones may imagine a futuristic device that humans implant in themselves to convert the calories they consume into electricity for their personal devices – i.e., a dietary and electricity-producing device in one! Students may dream of a home electrical system that not only uses wind and solar energy to power a home but one that uses a combination of devices that recaptures loss energy (e.g., heat, kinetic, etc.). The number of options for the final project is vast, and this lesson is geared towards getting the students' minds on a grand, imaginative track that will guide them towards their final, innovative product.

You should be familiar with 1st, 2nd, and 3rd generation renewable/sustainable energy sources, and in particular, you should be familiar with photovoltaic cells and solar energy technologies. The following are useful resources:

- "How solar panels work" - *www.youtube.com/watch?v=dngqYjHfr98)*

- "The Power of the Sun – The Science of the Silicon Solar Cell" - *www.youtube.com/watch?v=u0hckM8TKY0*

- Multi-generational energy sources – *www.en.wikipedia.org/wiki/Sustainable_energy*

- Future generations of energy - *www.youtube.com/watch?v=uStFvcz9Or4*

- Ten future energy sources: *www.youtube.com/watch?v=uStFvcz9Or4*

Solar panels are made of many photovoltaic cells working together. Each cell creates an electric field when opposite charges are forced to separate. To make charges separate to create electricity, makers of photovoltaic cells take a semi-conducting material like silicon, and create two layers. They seed phosphorus on the top layer, creating a positive charge (extra electrons), and seed the bottom layer with boron, creating a negative charge (fewer electrons). When the sun shines on these layers, the photons that hit the layers knock an electron free into the surrounding metal plates that are between each of the cells. These plate conduct the electric potential and work just as wires, then the electricity can be used as any other source of electricity.

Fossil Fuels

Fossil fuels are non-renewable, polluting sources of energy. You should be prepared to support the develop of students' understanding of how intricately oil is woven into the world's economy and how it has affected life around the globe in the past (for example, the 1973 U.S. oil crisis) and present (for example, oil market fluctuations and associated global economy impacts) as well possibilities of the future. Be prepared to encourage students to ponder the impact a drastic drop in demand for oil would have on the world's economy or what would happen if we ran out of oil without alternatives that could maintain future energy demands.

A number of issues impact individuals' reasons for hesitating to adopt renewable/sustainable energies in lieu of fossil fuels. Be prepared to address the concerns of these individuals and help students devise ways to persuade them view renewable/sustainable energies from a variety of perspectives.

One way to help students see an issue from multiple perspectives is use the Six Thinking Hats activity. In this activity, five colored hats are a frame for students thinking critically in five different ways.

Color of "hat"	Perspective
Blue	Management - What is the goal and how to we plan to achieve it?
White	Information processing – What do we know about this? How do we make sense of new information?
Black	Practical – What are the possible reasons to be cautious and conservative?
Yellow	Optimistic – What are the benefits of this issues?
Green	Creative – What provocations or questions can be asked about this issue?

By assigning different "hats" to students, and having them discuss the issue with that particular perspective, students can see different facets of an issue.

Engineering Design Process

In this lesson, students are challenged to work in teams to investigate the energy production of photovoltaic cells. They will use the engineering design process (EDP), the same process that professional engineers use in their work, to structure their group investigation. A graphic representation of the EDP is provided at the end of this lesson. It may be useful to post this in your classroom.

The EDP is a cyclical process consisting of a number of steps that are iterative in nature:

- Identify the problem

- Brainstorm ideas and conduct background research

- Create a plan (e.g., by sketching designs, formulating processes)

- Build (this may mean building an object or formulating a process or solution)

- Test

- Redesign

- Share solutions

The following website provides additional information about the EDP: *www.pbs learningmedia.org/resource/phy03.sci.engin.design.desprocess/what-is-the-engineering-design-process.*

COMMON MISCONCEPTIONS

Students will have various types of prior knowledge about the concepts introduced in this lesson. Table 4.6 outlines some common misconceptions students may have

concerning these concepts. Because of the breadth of students' experiences, it is not possible to anticipate every misconception that students may bring as they approach this lesson. Incorrect or inaccurate prior understanding of concepts can influence student learning in the future, however, so it is important to be alert to misconceptions such as those presented in the table.

Table 4.6. Common Misconceptions About the Concepts in Lesson 2

Topic	Student Misconception	Explanation
Energy	Renewable energy can only work on a small scale.	Renewable energy can be used for large-scale electricity generation. For example, Iceland generates most of its energy using renewable sources, using geothermal and hydroelectric power plants (source: *www.clickenergy.com.au/news-blog/12-countries-leading-the-way-in-renewable-energy/*)
	Energy can be created.	Energy is not created, but it can change forms. Electricity is the result of energy stored, for example, in fossil fuels, light, and the wind being transformed into energy that can be used for specific purposes by humans.
	Since fossil fuels come from dead plants and animals, they are renewable resources.	It takes millions of years for plant and animal remains to turn into fossil fuels. Because this process is too slow to replenish what we use as we use it, fossil fuels are not considered renewable resources.
Engineering Design Process (EDP)	Engineers use only the scientific process to solve problems in their work.	The scientific method is used to test predictions and explanations about the world. The EDP, on the other hand, is used to create a solution to a problem through testing and redesign. In reality, engineers use both processes (see Teacher Background section in Lesson 2 for more information about the differences and similarities between the scientific method and the EDP).

PREPARATION FOR LESSON 2

Review the Teacher Background Information provided (p. 25), assemble the materials for the lesson, and preview the videos and websites recommended in the Learning Plan Components section below. You should be prepared to list the various renewable/sustainable energy sources students research, and guide classes to finding others they may not identify easily. For example, if no one in the class identifies hydrogen fuel cells as an energy source, you should be ready to point the class towards sites related to hydrogen fuel cells.

LEARNING PLAN COMPONENTS
Introductory Activity/Engagement

Connection to the Challenge: Begin each day of this lesson by reminding students of the module challenge and directing students' attention to the question "How can electricity be generated in a renewable/sustainable way for use in everyday life?" Follow up by asking questions such as:

- Do we depend on other countries?

- How can we be sure that we will have consistent energy sources for as long as the earth is populated by humans?

Hold a brief student discussion of how their learning in the previous days' lesson(s) contributed to their ability to create their innovation for the final challenge. You may wish to hold a class discussion, creating a class list of key ideas on chart paper or the board, or you may wish to have students create a STEM Research Notebook entry with this information.

Science Class: Show students a video about cutting-edge and futuristic energy sources such as "Top10 Future Energy Sources" *www.youtube.com/watch?v=uStFvcz9Or4*. Hold a class discussion about the feasibility of these technologies. Next, guide students to internet sources on sustainable energy, solar thermal energy, and the smart grid and have them explore the different forms of renewable/sustainable energy sources, taking notes in their STEM Research Notebooks on each energy source and topic they explore. Examples of sources include:

- Solar Thermal: https://en.wikipedia.org/wiki/Solar_thermal

- Smart Grid: https://en.wikipedia.org/wiki/Smart_grid

- Hot dry rock geothermal energy: https://en.wikipedia.org/wiki/Hot_dry_rock_geothermal_energy

- Ocean Energy: https://en.wikipedia.org/wiki/Ocean_energy

- Biomass gasification: https://en.wikipedia.org/wiki/Biomass_gasification

- Hydropower: https://en.wikipedia.org/wiki/Hydropower

- Biomass: https://en.wikipedia.org/wiki/Biomass

- Geothermal power: https://en.wikipedia.org/wiki/Geothermal_power

- Solar Heating: https://en.wikipedia.org/wiki/Solar_heating

- Wind power: https://en.wikipedia.org/wiki/Wind_power

Students should use these pages as a starting point for finding other forms of renewable or sustainable energy sources. Teachers should also instruct students to look for web pages related to energy efficiency and recapturing heat.

Mathematics Connection: Have students complete the STEM Research Notebook Prompt below.

STEM Research Notebook Prompt

Watch the video, "The Basics of Electricity – What is an Amp" at *www.youtube.com/watch?v=8gvJzrjwjds&list=PL253772980E9A0F88&index=1*.

In your STEM Research Notebook, take notes on the massive numbers involved in powering something as simple as a smartphone, then answer this question:

How might you explain to someone on the street how many electrons are involve in powering a smartphone?

ELA Connection: Have students respond to the STEM Research Notebook prompt below.

STEM Research Notebook Prompt

Answer the following questions in your STEM Research Notebook:

- Do you believe everyone in the U.S. wants to switch to renewable/sustainable energy sources? If so, why? If not, why not?

- What are the Pros and Cons of switching to renewable/sustainable energy sources?

Hold a class discussion about students' opinions about renewable/sustainable energy sources and the costs of pursuing alternatives to fossil fuels.

Social Studies Connection: Ask students to consider what would happen if the world's oil supply was cut off. Hold a class discussion in which students share their ideas, then show them the footage from an NBC News segment about the OPEC's 1973 embargo found at *www.youtube.com/watch?v=VCLRlVxOH-Q*, and pictures of what occurred

after the embargo was set in motion (for example, *www.google.com/search?q=1973+oil+ crisis&source=lnms&tbm=isch&sa=X&ved=0CAcQ_AUoAWoVChMIgq2WwaSPxwIVhc2 ACh0P2gVO&biw=1280&bih=623*.

Next, have students research the embargo, responding to the STEM Research Notebook prompt below.

STEM Research Notebook Prompt

Research about OPEC's 1973 oil embargo to answer the following questions:

- What does the OPEC organization do? Why was it formed?

- What were the factors that led up to OPEC's embargo? Why did they decide to stop exporting oil?

- What impact did the embargo have on daily life in the U.S.? What evidence do you have to support your answer?

Activity/Exploration

Science Class: Students will write a three-page essay on a specific renewable/sustainable energy source. environment. Hold a class discussion, asking students to name the renewable/sustainable energy sources they identified in the Introductory Activity/ Engagement, and give a brief description of each. List each energy source on the board and have each student choose one source to research. Students should read/watch at least five sources for their energy sources and write a paper thoroughly describing how it works, the energy it produces, and its potential for contributing to the world's power needs (remind students that one energy source does not need to power the entire world, just contribute to a portion of its energy needs).

The paper must include the following content:

1. A thorough explanation of how the technology works, citing at least four sources

2. The average energy output of one unit (e.g., a single solar panel, one windmill, etc.) of the technology

    a. What that energy output means in regards to powering houses

3. An estimate (with data to back it up) of the percentage of the world's power needs that can be generated from the technology if scaled up (used in far greater number than it is presently) to a mass market

4. An explanation of the impact a scaled-up version of the technology would have on the environment.

Mathematics Connection: Have students conduct Internet research to find the outputs of various energy sources and have them conjecture what the values mean in terms of the number of houses the energy sources can power. For example in 2017, average US residential utility consumption was 10,399 kilowatthours, the lowest annual electricity consumption by state was in Hawaii (6,074 kWh) and the highest was Louisiana at 14,242 kWh. Average energy output information can be found at the U.S. Energy Information Administration – https://www.eia.gov/tools/faqs/faq.php?id= 97&t=3.

Then, have students compare the amount of energy created at large power plants (coal, nuclear, hydroelectric, etc.) to the energy demands of the world. Students can use this type of table in their STEM Research Notebook to record their findings from Internet research.

Type of energy source	Percentage of energy
Coal	41%
Oil	5%
Natural gas	20%
Hydroelectric	14%
Wind	1%
Geothermal	2%
Solar	2%
Nuclear power	12%
Biofuels and biomass	3%

Source: Institute for Energy Research https://www.instituteforenergyresearch.org/

ELA Connection: Have students work in groups of 3–4 students and respond to the STEM Research Notebook prompt below.

STEM Research Notebook Prompt

Brainstorm with your group and record ideas for convincing the following people to buy solar panels for their home: (a) A member of the Green Party who owns a single family home in a metropolitan area; (b) A farmer in Nebraska; and (c) A member of the Tea Party living in a suburb of San Francisco.

Share your ideas with one other group.

4 Rebuilding the Natural Environment Lesson Plans

Social Studies Connection: Have students research the evolution of the oil industry since the crises in the 1970s and write a two-page paper on how it has impacted the U.S. and world's economy.

Explanation

Science Class: Have students conduct internet research to find out the process photovoltaic cells undergo to create electricity and respond to the STEM Research Notebook prompt below.

STEM Research Notebook Prompt

Write an explanation to an audience of 7th graders how photovoltaic cells convert light energy to electricity. Include diagrams in your explanations.

Then answer the following question:

If a household's electricity is powered only by photovoltaic cells, will they have consistent electricity even on a rainy day?

Mathematics Connection: Ask students how electricity is measured on their home electricity bills. Introduce the idea that electricity is measured in kilowatt hours, and that 1 kilowatt is equal to 1,000 watts, so 1 kilowatt hour is an hour of electricity use at 1,000 watts. Refer students to *www.rapidtables.com/convert/electric/watt-to-kwh.html* for information about converting watts to kilowatt hours and have students work through several sample problems (e.g., what is the consumption in kilowatt hours for an appliance that uses 2500 watts over 2 hours).

Show students how to calculate the energy output of a personal and home solar system and determine what portion of a household can be powered by such a source of energy. Solar panels for homes are typically 5.5 feet tall and 3 feet wide. One solar panel can produce 320 watts which will power 5.33 60-watt bulbs. To calculate the solar panel output per day, students can use this formula:

320 Watt (from solar panel) X number of hours of full sun per day = energy per day

Students can look up how much full sun they get per day on Weather Underground's solar calculator – https://www.wunderground.com/calculators/solar.html

To find out how much one solar panel will produce in a month, take the energy generated per day and multiply by 30. Students can then compare this energy output with the electricity bill for the month to determine how much of their energy demands can be satisfied with one panel. Challenge students to consider how many solar panels they can place in a reasonable area of their home rooftop to calculate the maximum amount of energy output by solar means.

NATIONAL SCIENCE TEACHING ASSOCIATION

ELA Connection: Hold a class discussion about persuasive writing, asking students to provide examples of places where they have seen persuasive writing used and asking them to provide examples of types of language used in persuasive writing. Tell students that persuasive writing is a key aspect of advertising. Have students respond to the STEM Research Notebook prompt below.

STEM Research Notebook Prompt

Examine the images of advertisements found by searching for images on the internet using the search terms "persuasive advertising."

Choose three images that use both images and text and describe what the advertisement is selling. Answer the following questions:

How did the advertisement try to persuade the potential customer?

Why were these advertisements compelling to you?

Social Studies Connection: Explain the basic tenets of supply and demand and how they pertain to the oil industry, with an emphasis on how principles of supply and demand give OPEC significant influence over the world economies. Hold a class discussion about how the manipulation of oil supply and demand has shaped the pursuit of renewable/sustainable energy sources.

Elaboration/Application of Knowledge

Science Class: Have students work in teams to investigate the energy production of photovoltaic cells by using galvanometers to measure the energy output of these cells when subjected to varying intensities of light and angles of cells to light source. Their goal will be to create the maximum electricity output for a combination of intensity of light and position of light.

Students who need some support with this activity can use the following set of tables to test each variable and then combine them to provide evidence for the greatest position and intensity of light for solar energy production.

Table 4.7. Testing the angle of the photovoltaic cell on energy output

Angle of photovoltaic cell measured from a horizontal surface	Trials of Energy output from galvanometer				
30 degrees from horizontal					
40 degrees from horizontal					

Continued

Table 4.7. (*continued*)

Angle of photovoltaic cell measured from a horizontal surface	Trials of Energy output from galvanometer				
50 degrees from horizontal					
60 degrees from horizontal					
70 degrees from horizontal					
80 degrees from horizontal					
90 degrees from horizontal					
Angle with most energy output:					

Table 4.8. Testing the intensity of light on the output of a photovoltaic cell

Wattage of lightbulb (lumens)	Trials of Energy output from galvanometer				
30 W (400 lumens)					
40W (600 lumens)					
50W (750 lumens)					
60W (900 lumens)					
100W (1600 lumens)					
Bulb intensity with most energy output:					

To test the two variables together for maximum energy output, students should choose the angle AND bulb intensity with the most energy output, and test the range higher and lower than those choices to see if it does indeed give the maximum energy output together. For example, if 40 degrees and 60W were the highest energy output, then students should test the following variables for possible combinations around the maximum: 30 degrees, 40 degrees and 50 degrees; 50W, 60W and 100W.

Students should use the Engineering Design Process (EDP) to structure their investigation. Introduce the EDP to students as a process by which engineers and other STEM professionals solve problems and accomplish complex tasks. Emphasize to students

Table 4.9. Testing the highest output of angle and intensity of light on the output of a photovoltaic cell

Angle of photovoltaic cell measured from a horizontal surface	Wattage of lightbulb (lumens)	Trials of Energy output from galvanometer				
Highest output: 40 degrees from horizontal	50W (750 lumens)					
Highest output: 40 degrees from horizontal	60W (900 lumens)					
Highest output: 40 degrees from horizontal	100W (1600 lumens)					
30 degrees from horizontal	50W (750 lumens)					
30 degrees from horizontal	60W (900 lumens)					
30 degrees from horizontal	100W (1600 lumens)					
50 degrees from horizontal	50W (750 lumens)					
50 degrees from horizontal	60W (900 lumens)					
50 degrees from horizontal	100W (1600 lumens)					
Angle and bulb intensity with most energy output:						

that engineers routinely work collaboratively and that they will work as teams to solve their final challenge. The EDP will provide a framework for this group work. Show students the EDP graphic (attached at the end of this lesson) and review each of the steps with students. As they plan and create their models, they should note their progress in their STEM Research Notebooks by creating an entry for each stage of the EDP for the development of the description of the simulation.

Students should provide evidence of their use of the EDP in their STEM Research Notebooks, labeling a page with each step of the EDP and providing information appropriate to that step. You may wish to provide students with a general outline for organizing this information in their notebooks. For example:

1. Define

   a. What is the goal of your investigation?

   b. What products do you need to produce?

2. Learn

    a. What additional information do you need?
    b. What did you find out from your research? Remember to provide citations for your information.
    c. What ideas do team members have?

3. Plan

    a. How will you schedule your work to ensure that you complete it on time?
    b. How will you divide tasks? Hint: you might want to create a chart assigning team members jobs.
    c. What materials do you need?

4. Try

    a. Create the components of your response

        i.   Goal of investigation
        ii. Written description of investigation
        iii. Data table for investigation

5. Test

    a. Test out your light intensities and positions
    b. What worked well?
    c. What didn't work well?

6. Decide

    a. Based upon your test run(s) of your investigation, what will you change?

7. Share

    a. Share your investigation results in a whole class – make sure you know who will present various parts of your presentation of your investigation

Mathematics Connection: Have students use scientific notation to determine the number of electrons in a kilowatt hour based on the figure determined in the Activity/Exploration portion of this lesson. Student should research other measures of electricity and power (e.g., watts, amps, Coulombs, Joules, etc.) to gain a sufficient understanding. As stated earlier, in 2017, average US residential utility consumption was 10,399 kilowatthours, the lowest annual electricity consumption by state was in Hawaii (6,074 kWh) and the highest was Louisiana at 14,242 kWh. Average energy output information can be found at the U.S. Energy Information Administration – https://www.eia.gov/tools/faqs/faq.php?id=97&t=3.

1 Joule of energy = 1 Watt-Second, therefore 1kWh = 3.6 x10^6 Joules

1 kWh = 2.3 x 102^5 electronVolts

Electron Volts is the unit of energy equal to the work done on an electron to accelerate it through the potential of 1 volt.

ELA Connection: Have students write letters to their parents or caregivers about the potential benefits of using solar panels in their homes. Encourage students to share their letters with parents or caregivers and invite responses.

Social Studies Connection: Have students research the history of power struggles and wars based on gas and oil. Have each student in the class research one event, possibly from the list of examples below, and then form a classroom timeline of these events. Have students write a paragraph about the trends they see in the timeline and their thoughts about the destruction that these conflicts have caused. The following article may incite debate and get students thinking about the subject: *www.alternet.org/ story/155372/6_global_conflicts_that_have_flared_up_over_oil_and_gas*

Arguably, all of these events were related to securing oil resources:

World War I (1914–1919)
Events before Pearl Harbor attack (1941)
World War II (1939–1945)
Nigerian Civil War (1967–1970)
Iran-Iraq War (1980–1988)
Gulf War (1990–1991)
Iraq War (2003–2011)
Heglig Crisis – South Sudan- Sudan border conflict (2012)
Syrian Civil War (2015-present)

Evaluation/Assessment

Students may be assessed on the following performance tasks and other measures listed.

Performance Tasks

- Paper on Sustainable/Renewable Energy Sources

- Photovoltaic Cell Investigation

Other Measures

- STEM Research Notebook prompts
- Participation in class discussions

INTERNET RESOURCES

Sustainable energy background resources

- *www.youtube.com/watch?v=dngqYjHfr98)*
- *www.youtube.com/watch?v=u0hckM8TKY0*
- *www.en.wikipedia.org/wiki/Sustainable_energy*
- *www.youtube.com/watch?v=uStFvcz9Or4*
- *www.youtube.com/watch?v=uStFvcz9Or4*

EDP

- *www.pbslearningmedia.org/resource/phy03.sci.engin.design.desprocess/what-is-the-engineering-design-process.*

Countries using renewable energy

- *www.clickenergy.com.au/news-blog/12-countries-leading-the-way-in-renewable-energy/)*

Examples of renewable energy sources

- *www.en.wikipedia.org/wiki/Smart_grid*
- *www.en.wikipedia.org/wiki/Hot_dry_rock_geothermal_energy*
- *www.en.wikipedia.org/wiki/Ocean_energy*
- *www.en.wikipedia.org/wiki/Biomass_gasification*
- *www.en.wikipedia.org/wiki/Hydropower*
- *www.en.wikipedia.org/wiki/Biomass*
- *www.en.wikipedia.org/wiki/Geothermal_power*
- *www.en.wikipedia.org/wiki/Solar_heating*
- *www.en.wikipedia.org/wiki/Wind_power*

What is an amp

- *www.youtube.com/watch?v=8gvJzrjwjds&list=PL253772980E9A0F88&index=1*

OPEC Oil embargo

- *www.youtube.com/watch?v=VCLRlVxOH-Q*

- *www.google.com/search?q=1973+oil+crisis&source=lnms&tbm=isch&sa=X&ved= 0CAcQ_AUoAWoVChMIgq2WwaSPxwIVhc2ACh0P2gVO&biw=1280&bih=623*

Energy unit conversions

- *www.rapidtables.com/convert/electric/watt-to-kwh.html*

Conflicts over oil and gas

- *www.alternet.org/story/155372/6_global_conflicts*

Rubric for Paper on Sustainable Energy

	Expert (4)	Competent (3)	Emerging (2)	Did not meet expectations (1)	Score
Description of the Energy Source Comments	The student's description makes it clear that s/he thoroughly research the topic. The quality of the description makes it easy for a 10-year-old to understand how the technology works and there are at least four sources cited	The student's description makes it clear that s/he researched the topic well. The quality of the description makes it easy for a 15-year-old to understand how the technology works. There are four sources cited	The description of the energy source is not incredibly clear, and there are one or two key aspects of the technology that were not discussed. There are only three sources cited	The student clearly did not research the energy source thoroughly. There is only one or two sources cited, and the quality of the description is poor	
Energy Output Comments	The energy output was obviously researched, as it is accurate. The number of houses a single unit of the source can power checks out	The energy output is accurate. A number is given for the number of houses a single unit can power, but a source for checking it is not given	The energy output is given, but the number of houses a single unit can power is not determined.	The energy output is inaccurate and the number of houses a single unit can power is not given.	
Scaled-up Energy Calculation Comments	The scaled up calculation is accurate and realistically considers the number of units that can be truly used throughout the world. Also, the student considers the present power consumption of the world, the percentage of power drawn presently from the energy source, and the new figure if it were scaled up.	The scaled up calculation is accurate and realistically considers the number of units that can be truly used throughout the world. The student considers the present power consumption of the world, but does not consider the percentage of power drawn presently from the energy source, when calculating a new figure for energy production after the source has been scaled up.	The scaled up calculation is inaccurate or does not realistically consider the number of units that can be truly used throughout the world. The student considers the present power consumption of the world, but does not consider the percentage of power drawn presently from the energy source, when calculating a new figure for energy production after the source has been scaled up.	The scaled up calculation is inaccurate and does not realistically consider the number of units that be truly be used throughout the world. No calculation for the amount of energy it would produce if scaled up is given.	

Rubric for Paper on Sustainable Energy

	Expert (4)	Competent (3)	Emerging (2)	Did not meet expectations (1)	Score
Explanation of Environmental Impact Comments	The student gives a thorough explanation of the environmental impact of the scaled up version of the energy source and considers every aspect (e.g., amount of land used, possible threat to animals, etc.) the energy source can have on the environment.	The student gives a thorough explanation of the environmental impact of the scaled up version of the energy source but does not consider every impact (e.g., amount of land used, possible threat to animals, etc.) the energy source can have on the environment.	The explanation is not thorough and leaves out at least one significant impact the energy source can have on the environment.	The explanation is poor and leaves out two or more significant impacts the energy source can have on the environment.	
Total Score:					

Lesson Plan 3

GETTING OFF THE GRID

In this lesson, students will determine the cost-effectiveness of taking a single-family home off the current electrical grid and powering it solely from available renewable/sustainable energy sources. Students will consider the energy outputs of the sources they use and the effects of weather on those outputs. Students will also consider costs relative to energy savings, and will create brochures promoting their choice to various audiences.

ESSENTIAL QUESTIONS

- What is the average energy consumption of different household around the world in comparison to the U.S. households?

- How can we calculate the number of kilowatt-hours an energy source generates based on its power output?

- What are viable alternative energy sources for home?

- What is the importance of energy storage when using renewable/sustainable energy sources for home power?

ESTABLISHED GOALS AND OBJECTIVES

At the conclusion of this lesson, students will be able to do the following:

- Identify the power output of an energy source and calculate the number of kilowatt-hours it produces.

- Estimate the number of hours an energy source can generate electricity based on environmental conditions (e.g., sunlight for solar, wind for windmills, etc.).

- Analyze a system of renewable/sustainable energy sources that can supply a minimum of 100% of a household's energy needs.

- Identify several ways to make a home more energy efficient (e.g., dual-pane windows, insulation, etc.).

TIME REQUIRED

- 4 days (approximately 45 minutes per day; see Tables 3.8–3.9, pp. 40–41)

MATERIALS

Required Materials for Lesson 3

- Computers with internet connection

CONTENT STANDARDS AND KEY VOCABULARY

Table 4.10 lists the content standards from the *Next Generation Science Standards (NGSS), Common Core State Standards,* and the Framework for 21st Century Learning that this lesson addresses, and Table 4.11 presents the key vocabulary. Vocabulary terms are provided for both teacher and student use. Teachers may choose to introduce some or all of the terms to students.

Table 4.10. Standards Addressed in STEM Road Map Module Lesson Three

NEXT GENERATION SCIENCE STANDARDS

PERFORMANCE EXPECTATIONS

- HS-LS2–7. Design, evaluate, and refine a solution for reducing the impacts of human activities on the environment and biodiversity.
- HS-ETS1–3. Evaluate a solution to a complex real-world problem based on prioritized criteria and trade-offs that account for a range of constraints, including cost, safety, reliability, and aesthetics as well as possible social, cultural, and environmental impacts.

DISCIPLINARY CORE IDEAS

LS2.C. Ecosystem Dynamics, Functioning, and Resilience

- Anthropogenic changes (induced by human activity) in the environment – including habitat destruction, pollution, introduction of invasive species, overexploitation, and climate change – can disrupt an ecosystem and threaten the survival of some species.

LS4.D. Biodiversity and Humans

- Biodiversity is increased by the formation of new species (speciation) and decreased by the loss of species (extinction). (secondary)
- Humans depend on the living world for the resources and other benefits provided by biodiversity. But human activity is also having adverse impacts on biodiversity through overpopulation, overexploitation, habitat destruction, pollution, introduction of invasive species, and climate change. Thus sustaining biodiversity so that ecosystem functioning and productivity are maintained is essential to supporting and enhancing life on Earth. Sustaining biodiversity also aids humanity by preserving landscapes of recreational or inspirational value.

Continued

Table 4.10 (*continued*)

ETS1.A. Defining and Delimiting an Engineering Problem

- Criteria and constraints also include satisfying any requirements set by society, such as taking issues of risk mitigation into account, and they should be quantified to the extent possible and stated in such a way that one can tell if a given design meets them.

ETS1.B. Developing Possible Solutions

- When evaluating solutions it is important to take into account a range of constraints including cost, safety, reliability and aesthetics and to consider social, cultural and environmental impacts.

CROSSCUTTING CONCEPTS

Stability and Change

- Much of science deals with constructing explanations of how things change and how they remain stable.

Connections to Engineering, Technology, and Applications of Science

- Influence of science, engineering and technology on society and the natural world
- Modern civilization depends on major technological systems. Engineers continuously modify these technological systems by applying scientific knowledge and engineering design practices to increase benefits while decreasing costs and risks.

COMMON CORE STATE STANDARDS FOR MATHEMATICS

MATHEMATICAL PRACTICES

- MP1. Make sense of problems and persevere in solving them.
- MP3. Construct viable arguments and critique the reasoning of others.
- MP5. Use appropriate tools strategically.
- MP6. Attend to precision.
- MP7. Look for and make use of structure.
- MP8. Look for and express regularity in repeated reasoning.
- MP8. Look for and express regularity in repeated reasoning.

MATHEMATICAL CONTENT

- BF.A.1.a. Determine an explicit expression, a recursive process, or steps for calculation from a context.
- CED.A.1. Create equations and inequalities in one variable and use them to solve problems.
- CED.A.2. Create equations in two or more variables to represent relationships between quantities; graph equations on coordinate axes with labels and scales.
- REI.C.5 Prove that, given a system of two equations in two variables, replacing one equation by the sum of that equation and a multiple of the other produces a system with the same solutions.

- REI.C.6. Solve systems of linear equations exactly and approximately (e.g., with graphs), focusing on pairs of linear equations in two variables.
- REI.C.10. Understand that the graph of an equation in two variables is the set of all its solutions plotted in the coordinate plane, often forming a curve (which could be a line).
- REI.C.11. Explain why the x-coordinates of the points where the graphs of the equations $y = f(x)$ and $y = g(x)$ intersect are the solutions of the equation $f(x) = g(x)$; find the solutions approximately, e.g., using technology to graph the functions, make tables of values, or find successive approximations.
- REI.C.12. Graph the solutions to a linear inequality in two variables as a half- plane (excluding the boundary in the case of a strict inequality), and graph the solution set to a system of linear inequalities in two variables as the intersection of the corresponding half-planes.
- IF.B.4. For a function that models a relationship between two quantities, interpret key features of graphs and tables in terms of the quantities, and sketch graphs showing key features given a verbal description of the relationship. Key features include intercepts; intervals where the function is increasing, decreasing, positive, or negative; relative maximums and minimums; symmetries; end behavior; and periodicity.
- IF.B.5. Relate the domain of a function to its graph and, where applicable, to the quantitative relationship it describes. For example, if the function h(n) gives the number of person-hours it takes to assemble n engines in a factory, then the positive integers would be an appropriate domain for the function.
- IF.B.6. Calculate and interpret the average rate of change of a function (presented symbolically or as a table) over a specified interval. Estimate the rate of change from a graph.

COMMON CORE STATE STANDARDS FOR ENGLISH LANGUAGE ARTS

WRITING STANDARDS

- W.9–10.1a-e Write arguments to support claims in an analysis of substantive topics or texts, using valid reasoning and relevant and sufficient evidence. Explore and inquire into areas of interest to formulate an argument.

    f) Introduce precise claim(s), distinguish the claim(s) from alternate or opposing claims, and create an organization that establishes clear relationships among claim(s), counterclaims, reasons, and evidence.
    g) Develop claim(s) and counterclaims fairly, supplying evidence for each while pointing out the strengths and limitations of both in a manner that anticipates the audience's knowledge level and concerns.
    h) Use words, phrases, and clauses to link the major sections of the text, create cohesion, and clarify the relationships between claim(s) and reasons, between reasons and evidence, and between claim(s) and counterclaims.
    i) Establish and maintain a formal style and objective tone while attending to the norms and conventions of the discipline in which they are writing.
    j) Provide a concluding statement or section that follows from and supports the argument presented.

Continued

Table 4.10 (*continued*)

- W.9–10.2a-f Write informative/explanatory texts to examine and convey complex ideas, concepts, and information clearly and accurately through the effective selection, organization, and analysis of content.

  a) Introduce a topic; organize complex ideas, concepts, and information to make important connections and distinctions; include formatting (e.g., headings), graphics (e.g., figures, tables), and multimedia when useful to aiding comprehension.
  b) Develop the topic with well-chosen, relevant, and sufficient facts, extended definitions, concrete details, quotations, or other information and examples appropriate to the audience's knowledge of the topic.
  c) Use appropriate and varied transitions to link the major sections of the text, create cohesion, and clarify the relationships among complex ideas and concepts.
  d) Use precise language and domain-specific vocabulary to manage the complexity of the topic.
  e) Establish and maintain a formal style and objective tone while attending to the norms and conventions of the discipline in which they are writing.
  f) Provide a concluding statement or section that follows from and supports the information or explanation presented (e.g., articulating implications or the significance of the topic).

- W.9–10.4 Produce clear and coherent writing in which the development, organization, and style are appropriate to task, purpose, and audience.
- W.9–10.5. Develop and strengthen writing as needed by planning, revising, editing, rewriting, or trying a new approach, focusing on addressing what is most significant for a specific purpose and audience.
- W.9–10.7. Conduct short as well as more sustained research projects to answer a question (including a self-generated question) or solve a problem; narrow or broaden the inquiry when appropriate; synthesize multiple sources on the subject, demonstrating understanding of the subject under investigation.
- W.9–10.8. Gather relevant information from multiple authoritative print and digital sources, using advanced searches effectively; assess the usefulness of each source in answering the research question; integrate information into the text selectively to maintain the flow of ideas, avoiding plagiarism and following a standard format for citation.
- W.9–10.9a-b. Draw evidence from literary or informational texts to support analysis, reflection, and research.
- Apply *grades 9–10 Reading standards* to literature (e.g., "Analyze how an author draws on and transforms source material in a specific work
- Apply *grades 9–10 Reading standards* to literary nonfiction (e.g., "Delineate and evaluate the argument and specific claims in a text, assessing whether the reasoning is valid and the evidence is relevant and sufficient; identify false statements and fallacious reasoning").
- W.9–10.10 Write routinely over extended time frames (time for research, reflection, and revision) and shorter time frames (a single sitting or a day or two) for a range of tasks, purposes, and audiences.

SPEAKING AND LISTENING STANDARDS

- SL.9–10.1a-d. Engage effectively in a range of collaborative discussions (one-on-one, in groups, and teacher-led) with diverse partners on *grade 10 topics, texts, and issues*, building on others' ideas and expressing their own clearly.

  k. Come to discussions prepared, having read or studied required material; explicitly draw on that preparation by referring to evidence on the topic, text, or issue to probe and reflect on ideas under discussion.
  l. Follow rules for collegial discussions, set specific goals and deadlines, and define individual roles as needed.
  m. Pose and respond to specific questions with elaboration and detail by making comments that contribute to the topic, text, or issue under discussion.
  n. Review the key ideas expressed and demonstrate understanding of multiple perspectives through reflection and paraphrasing.
  o. Seek to understand and communicate with individuals from different perspectives and cultural backgrounds.

- SL.9–10.2. Interpret information presented in diverse media and formats (e.g., visually, quantitatively, orally) and explain how it contributes to a topic, text, or issue under study.
- SL.9–10.4. Present claims and findings, sequencing ideas logically and using pertinent descriptions, facts, and details to accentuate main ideas or themes; use appropriate eye contact, adequate volume, and clear pronunciation.

FRAMEWORK FOR 21ST CENTURY LEARNING
Information Literacy; Media Literacy; ICT Literacy; Flexibility and Adaptability; Initiative and Self-Direction; Social and Cross Cultural Skills; Productivity and Accountability; Leadership and Responsibility

Table 4.11. Key Vocabulary in Lesson Three

Key Vocabulary	Definition
battery	a combination of two or more electrochemical cells that store electric charge and that convert chemical energy into electric energy
Bloom Box	a solid oxide fuel cell (SOFC) power generator made by Bloom Energy
geothermal energy	the thermal energy generated and stored in the Earth
hydrogen fuel cell	a device that converts the chemical energy from a fuel into electricity through a chemical reaction of positively charged hydrogen ions with oxygen or another oxidizing agent; different than batteries because they require a continuous source of fuel and oxygen or air to sustain the chemical reaction

Continued

Table 4.11 (*continued*)

Key Vocabulary	Definition
inverter	a device that changes direct current into alternating current
solar heating	a type of heating for residences or other buildings; requires a collector, often fastened to a roof or a wall facing the sun that heats a fluid that is either pumped or driven by natural convection
solar panel	A panel designed to absorb the sun's rays as a source of energy for generating electricity or heating

TEACHER BACKGROUND INFORMATION

In this lesson, students will work in teams to design home power systems that use a combination of renewable/sustainable energy sources to meet at least 100% (excess energy generated by the systems can be sold back to energy companies) of a U.S. household's needs. Students must shop for several different products presently available for commercial/home use and combine them into a single system. They must determine the total cost of the system and increase its price by a percentage sufficient to account for installation and profit. Finally, students must create two versions of a brochure to market their systems to different demographics (Green party, city dwellers, and global-warming deniers). The brochures will need to briefly describe how their system works, how the energy output is calculated, how its surplus electricity can be stored or sold back to the grid, the cost of the system with installation, and how long it will take for the system to pay for itself.

You should be familiar with how to calculate kWh based on the power output of an energy source.

For example, if an appliance is rated 700W, divide 700 by 1000 to get kilowatts (.7). Then multiply the kW for the appliance by the number of hours the appliance is used. For the purposes of this lesson, you should use an average U.S. household energy use of 909 kWh per month. You should also be familiar with common sources of household energy production (fossil fuels, solar, wind, etc.), their limitations, and means of storing energy. Furthermore, you should understand how energy from these sources is converted to the alternating current (AC) used in homes.

Fossil Fuels

At a fossil fuel power plant, coal, oil and gas are burned to convert water to steam. The steam turns a turbine which is connected to a generator to produce electricity.

Solar Panels

When sunlight hits a solar panel, the photons or packets of energy dislodge electrons from the solar cells which then create electric potential through the conducting metals attached to solar cells, producing electricity.

Wind Turbine

As the wind blows the wind turbine, the blades are pushed to rotate. As the turbine spins, it is attached to another turbine which is connected to a generator to produce electricity.

COMMON MISCONCEPTIONS

Students will have various types of prior knowledge about the concepts introduced in this lesson. Table 4.12 outlines some common misconceptions students may have concerning these concepts. Because of the breadth of students' experiences, it is not possible to anticipate every misconception that students may bring as they approach this lesson. Incorrect or inaccurate prior understanding of concepts can influence student learning in the future, however, so it is important to be alert to misconceptions such as those presented in the table.

Table 4.12. Common Misconceptions About the Concepts in Lesson 3

Topic	Student Misconception	Explanation
Home energy conservation	Leaving lights, computers, and other electric appliances turned on when you are not going to be away for very long is a good idea. Switching them on and off all the time wears them out more quickly, and also produces sudden power spikes that negate any supposed energy savings.	Switching sophisticated modern appliances and electrical devices on and off frequently will not reduce their life span, and any power surges that might occur are likely to be miniscule.
	Closing the vents in unoccupied rooms is a good way to conserve energy.	This sounds obvious, but it is wrong. Furnaces produce enough heat to fill their ductwork systems, and they will continue to do so regardless of whether every register in the house is open or closed. Closing a few of them will simply redirect all the heat into other rooms, and because such a move increases the overall air pressure in the system, it will force the furnace or heating unit to work harder, thereby causing it to wear out more quickly.

PREPARATION FOR LESSON 3

Review the Teacher Background Information provided (p. 94), and preview the videos and websites recommended in the Learning Plan Components section below. In order to check students' work and the viability of their systems, you must be prepared to sum the energy production of the units (total power for all sources). In order to do this, you should know how to calculate kWh from power output (measured in watts), and know the average wind and sun exposure for the region in which they live. The following resources provide wind and sun exposure data for various regions:

- *www.windustry.org/wind_resource_and_speeds*

- *www.solardirect.com/pv/systems/gts/gts-sizing-sun-hours.html*

LEARNING PLAN COMPONENTS
Introductory Activity/Engagement

Connection to the Challenge: Begin each day of this lesson by directing students' attention to the driving question for the module, asking "How can electricity be generated in a renewable/sustainable way for use in everyday life?" Remind students of the module challenge each day and hold a brief student discussion of how their learning in the previous days' lesson(s) contributed to their ability to create their innovation for the final challenge. You may wish to hold a class discussion, creating a class list of key ideas on chart paper or the board, or you may wish to have students create a STEM Research Notebook entry with this information.

Science Class and ELA Connection: Hold a class discussion about viewpoints on alternative energy sources. Point out to students that people in the U.S. and around the world have different viewpoints on energy sources. Ask students what energy source(s) they think are best for the health of the Earth, creating a class list of student ideas. Next, ask students for ideas about how they might convince others with different viewpoints to change their minds.

Introduce the idea that there are individuals who power their homes using alternative energy sources. Show the video about the Michael Strizki who powers his whole house and generates hydrogen gas with renewable/sustainable energy sources found at *www.youtube.com/watch?v=Vel9LH57RII* and have students respond to the STEM Research Notebook prompt below.

STEM Research Notebook Prompt

Michael Strizki's house cost $500,000. How might you be able to redesign his living conditions to make the project of converting to solar energy cheaper?

Tell students that in this lesson they will devise an alternative energy source for a residence and calculate its output and the amount of time it would take to recoup its costs with the energy savings realized. Next, tell students that they will create two versions of a brochure to market their systems to different demographic groups. Give some time for groups of students to research the demographics for their location, including voting patterns. Discuss the demographics of your local area with the whole class. Brainstorm what groups might not be present in your local area. Students should record these groups in their STEM Research Notebook for future use to target their brochures.

Mathematics Connection: Have students research online to identify the power consumption of average houses around the world using a website such as https://yearbook.enerdata.net/electricity/electricity-domestic-consumption-data.html. Students should also identify the power output of several renewable energy sources (e.g., small and large windmills, hydro-electric dams, solar farms, etc.). Have students record their findings in their STEM Research Notebooks. Later in the lesson, students will use this information to come up with a hypothesis on the optimal combination of types of energy sources and the energy needs for three different countries around the world.

Social Studies Connection: Hold a class discussion about what students believe would happen to the oil industry and the world's economy if all U.S. households immediately stopped using fossil fuels to power their homes.

Activity/Exploration

Science Class: To begin their home alternative energy source project, have students search the Internet for renewable/sustainable energy devices for homes and determine how much of each they can fit on/in/around their current home. Be sure to record the specifications of your current home (square feet of floor space, number of rooms, etc.). Research and record the way each device works, the needs of the device, and how devices can be used in conjunction with one another. Students should also research battery backup systems as well.

Students will need to research the energy outputs of devices, and use weather data to estimate the amount of time devices will be able to generate electricity, and conservatively calculate the kilowatt hours generated on average for a whole-home system. Furthermore, students will need to calculate the amount of time needed to pay off such a device in relation to the money they would save by not paying the utility companies for electricity. In the U.S., the Public Utility Regulatory Policy Act (PURPA) has mandated that surplus energy can be sold back to the utility companies. Citizens can purchase a bidirectional meter to sell surplus electricity back to the local electric company (see https://science.howstuffworks.com/environmental/energy/sell-electricity-back-grid.htm for more details).

Mathematics Connection: Have students calculate the average number of kilowatt-hours each device in their system is capable of generating Consider a series of solar panels that produces 400 watts. This value times the number of hours it is exposed to direct sunlight divided by 1000 gives the number of kWh it produces. Such a product can be found here: https://www.amazon.com/Renogy-Monocrystalline-Solar-Starter-Wanderer/dp/B00BSZUHRC/ref=sr_1_4?s=lawn-garden&ie=UTF8&qid=15 43950697&sr=1-4&refinements=p_n_feature_keywords_browse-bin%3A71072 80011

In order to do so, students must determine the average amount of sun and wind exposure their region gets and multiply this time by the power output (Watts) of solar and wind turbines used in their systems. They must sum these kWh with all others generated by other devices to determine if their systems create at least 909 kWh per month. Additionally, students will create a system of equations representing the cost of their systems (considering the possibility of selling energy back to the utilities) to the average monthly cost of drawing energy from the regional utility.

ELA Connection: Have students create their brochures based on the system they designed in science class and the calculations from the mathematics connection.

Brochures should explain the product system that they chose from science class and the number of Watts that this product can provide. Then students should use their calculations from mathematics class to explain how much power the product can produce per month. Students should attempt to convince their audience through this brochure of the percent of power that can be generated from their chosen system, so that people are persuaded to adopt this alternative energy source.

Social Studies Connection: Saudi Arabia's oil currently accounts for about 85% of the exported oil in the world, providing Saudi Arabia with 90% of its fiscal revenue. In 2003, Saudi Arabia was the 27th largest economy in the world, an in 2014 it is the 19th largest economy in the world. However, with the collapse in global oil prices, Saudi Arabia's economy has begun to slow. Have small groups of students research Saudi Arabia's oil exports (the International Monetary Fund site has multiple publications that have easy to read summaries, for example: https://www.imf.org/en/Publications/CR/Issues/2016/12/31/Saudi-Arabia-Selected-Issues-43343) and create a graph that analyzes a trend from 2000 until today. Have students predict what the future for Saudi Arabia may be based on the trend they found on their graph and explain it to the class.

Explanation

Science Class: Have students explore power inverters and energy surpluses using the STEM Research Notebook prompt below.

STEM Research Notebook Prompt

Conduct Internet research to explain how power inverters are used in home power systems to convert mechanical and solar energy to the 120 and 220 volt alternating currents used in households. Investigate and explain how a surplus of energy can be sold back to the local utility companies for a profit.

Some of the follow sites may be helpful:

U.S. Wind Exchange: http://apps2.eere.energy.gov/wind/windexchange/wind_resource_maps.asp?stateab=va

Smart Power Grids (1): http://www.scientificamerican.com/report/smart-electricity-grid/

Smart Power Grids (2): http://blogs.scientificamerican.com/plugged-in/the-u-s-power-grid-is-in-need-of-a-technology-upgrade/

Calculating home power usage: http://www.rapidtables.com/convert/electric/watt-to-kwh.htm

Tesla Powerball: http://www.teslamotors.com/powerwall

Bloom Box: https://www.youtube.com/watch?v=shkFDPI6kGE

Fuel Cell: https://www.youtube.com/watch?v=R15R54oZAdA

Mathematics Connection: Students may need assistance to understand how to combine factors such as sun and wind exposure and power output to determine how they influence power production. For students in Algebra I, teachers may need to explain how systems of equations are used to interpret the point in time where a renewable/sustainable, home-energy system becomes a better deal than drawing energy from a utility.

Have students create graphs showing the cost of the system versus the cost of drawing electricity from the grid for their brochures.

Some of the following websites may be helpful:

Converting to AC: https://en.wikipedia.org/wiki/Solar_inverter

Wind coverage: http://www.windustry.org/wind_resource_and_speeds

Sun coverage: http://www.solardirect.com/pv/systems/gts/gts-sizing-sun-hours.html

Man completely off the grid: https://www.youtube.com/watch?v=Vel9LH57RII

Average household power consumption: http://shrinkthatfootprint.com/average-household-electricity-consumption

ELA Connection: Hold a class discussion about how advertisers appeal to different demographic groups in advertising. For example, appealing to a person's love for saving the planet may not work with a person who is more concerned with saving money. However, if that person is concerned about U.S. dependency on foreign oil, then encouraging him/her to use a system that decreases that dependency may be a good motivator.

Social Studies Connection: Hold a class discussion about how relations between nations would be different if oil had not been a commodity with high demand. Have students respond to the STEM Research Notebook prompt below.

STEM Research Notebook Prompt

Considering the wars or hostile situations involving oil you have discussed and speculate how different the world would be if the wars or hostile situations had not taken place.

Elaboration/Application of Knowledge

Science Class and Mathematics class: Students should present their brochures to the class and conduct peer review. Ask the entire class to conduct a peer review, beginning by making notes during the brochure presentations in their STEM Research Notebooks. The following protocol should be used for the peer review:

1. A student gives his or her presentation.

2. Peer reviewers ask clarifying questions, and the presenting student responds.

3. Peer reviewers explain all positive responses to the prototype by starting each response with the phrase "I like . . .," while the presenting student listens and takes notes.

4. Peer reviewers explain all responses regarding potential improvements to the brochure by starting each response with the phrase "I wish . . .," while the presenting student listens and takes notes.

5. The presenting student responds to the peer review by summarizing his or her next steps in redesigning the brochure.

ELA Connection: Students should make the improvements suggested by the peer review in science and mathematics classes. Have students use Photoshop or some other multimedia platform to transform their brochures to a digital format.

Social Studies Connection: Have students write a section for a fictional history book written for a post-oil world, imagining a country or region that changed (for the better or worse) after a major drop in demand for oil.

Evaluation/Assessment

Students may be assessed on the following performance tasks and other measures listed.

Performance Tasks

- Design of Home Power System
- Design of Brochures for two different demographic groups

Other Measures

- STEM Research Notebook prompts
- Participation in class discussions

INTERNET RESOURCES

U.S. Wind Exchange: http://apps2.eere.energy.gov/wind/windexchange/wind_resource_maps.asp?stateab=va

Smart Power Grids (1): http://www.scientificamerican.com/report/smart-electricity-grid/

Smart Power Grids (2): http://blogs.scientificamerican.com/plugged-in/the-u-s-power-grid-is-in-need-of-a-technology-upgrade/

Calculating home power usage: http://www.rapidtables.com/convert/electric/watt-to-kwh.htm

Tesla Powerball: http://www.teslamotors.com/powerwall

Bloom Box: https://www.youtube.com/watch?v=shkFDPI6kGE

Fuel Cell: https://www.youtube.com/watch?v=R15R54oZAdA

Converting to AC: https://en.wikipedia.org/wiki/Solar_inverter

Wind coverage: http://www.windustry.org/wind_resource_and_speeds

Sun coverage: http://www.solardirect.com/pv/systems/gts/gts-sizing-sun-hours.html

Man completely off the grid: https://www.youtube.com/watch?v=Vel9LH57RII

Average household power consumption: http://shrinkthatfootprint.com/average-household-electricity-consumption

Rubric for Home Power System Design and Brochure

	Expert (4)	Competent (3)	Emerging (2)	Did not meet expectations (1)	Score
Design of the system Comments	The system is a realistic fusion of three or more energy sources (battery systems may be included in this figure). The sources fit well on an average single-family property, and all components that allow each energy source has been included in the system.	The system is a realistic fusion of three or more energy sources (battery systems may be included in this figure). The sources fit well on an average single-family property. There are components needed for the energy sources to work together that were not included in the design of the system.	The system uses only two energy sources or uses one that is not commercially available for home use. All other aspects of the design are adequate.	The system uses only one energy component and does not consider battery back up.	
Accuracy of mathematics used to determine energy output Comments	The system creates at least 100% of a U.S. household's energy, and the mathematics used to determine this is sound. Students used an accurate graph to show the point in time where the system will pay for itself	The system creates at least 100% of a U.S. household's energy, and the mathematics to determine this has few mistakes. Students' graph is accurate.	The system does not produce 100% of the energy needed for a U.S. household, and there are many mistakes in the mathematics. A graph is included with a few mistakes.	The system does not produce 100% of the energy needed for a U.S. household, and there are many mistakes in the mathematics. A graph is not included.	
Advertising to the different demographics Comments	Students clearly considered the needs and motivations of both demographics and appealed to both sides respectfully and wisely.	Students considered the needs and motivations of both demographics and appealed to both sides respectfully and wisely but left out key, motivating facts one or both parties would have found useful	Students considered the needs and motivations of both demographics and appealed to both sides but demonstrated bias (e.g., conveyed sarcasm or sanctimony)	Students did not consider the needs or motivations one or both demographics	

Rubric for Home Power System Design and Brochure

	Expert (4)	Competent (3)	Emerging (2)	Did not meet expectations (1)	Score
Quality of the brochure Comments	The brochure is professional, includes all necessary information, and is aesthetically pleasing	The brochure is professional, includes most necessary information, and is aesthetically pleasing	The brochure lacks a professional appeal but has most of the necessary information for prospective buyers	The brochure is haphazardly constructed and is missing key pieces of information	
Total Score					

Lesson Plan 4

POWERING THE WORLD

In this lesson, students apply the knowledge and skills they learned in the previous lessons to create their own innovative, renewable/sustainable energy source. Students will work in teams to consider all aspects of a technology that could move the world away from dependence on fossil fuels. The technology may be as creative as the students wish, but students must be able to justify its foundation in science, and it must be able meet the energy needs.

ESSENTIAL QUESTIONS

- What innovative energy sources could meet the world's energy demands?

- How would a change in the way the world produces electricity impact the world ecologically and economically?

- How can we convince people to use cleaner, safer energy?

ESTABLISHED GOALS AND OBJECTIVES

At the conclusion of this lesson, students will be able to do the following:

- Apply their understanding of energy sources to propose an innovative renewable/sustainable energy source

- Calculate the percentage of the world's energy demand a renewable/sustainable energy source covers

- Make cogent arguments for the development of renewable/sustainable energy sources

- Identify the ecological impact of a large-scale renewable/sustainable energy source

- Identify the economic impact of a large-scale renewable/sustainable energy source

TIME REQUIRED

- 6 days (approximately 45 minutes per day; see Tables 3.9–3.10, pp. 41–42)

MATERIALS
Required Materials for Lesson 3

- Computers with internet connection and software for creating presentations and brochures

CONTENT STANDARDS AND KEY VOCABULARY

Table 4.13 lists the content standards from the *Next Generation Science Standards (NGSS), Common Core State Standards,* and the Framework for 21st Century Learning that this lesson addresses, and Table 4.14 presents the key vocabulary. Vocabulary terms are provided for both teacher and student use. Teachers may choose to introduce some or all of the terms to students.

Table 4.13. Standards Addressed in STEM Road Map Module Lesson 4

NEXT GENERATION SCIENCE STANDARDS
PERFORMANCE EXPECTATIONS
• HS-ETS1–3. Evaluate a solution to a complex real-world problem based on prioritized criteria and trade-offs that account for a range of constraints, including cost, safety, reliability, and aesthetics as well as possible social, cultural, and environmental impacts.
DISCIPLINARY CORE IDEAS
ETS1.A. Defining and Delimiting an Engineering Problem
• Criteria and constraints also include satisfying any requirements set by society, such as taking issues of risk mitigation into account, and they should be quantified to the extent possible and stated in such a way that one can tell if a given design meets them. (secondary)
ETS1.B. Developing Possible Solutions
• When evaluating solutions it is important to take into account a range of constraints including cost, safety, reliability and aesthetics and to consider social, cultural and environmental impacts.
CROSSCUTTING CONCEPTS
Energy and Matter
• Changes of energy and matter in a system can be described in terms of energy and matter flows into, out of, and within that system.
Stability and Change
• Much of science deals with constructing explanations of how things change and how they remain stable.
Connections to Engineering, Technology, and Applications of Science
• Influence of science, engineering and technology on society and the natural world
• Modern civilization depends on major technological systems. Engineers continuously modify these technological systems by applying scientific knowledge and engineering design practices to increase benefits while decreasing costs and risks.

Continued

Table 4.13 (*continued*)

SCIENCE AND ENGINEERING PRACTICES

Constructing Explanations and Designing Solutions

- Constructing explanations and designing solutions in 9–12 builds on K–8 experiences and progresses to explanations and designs that are supported by multiple and independent student-generated sources of evidence consistent with scientific ideas, principles, and theories.
- Design, evaluate, and/or refine a solution to a complex real-world problem, based on scientific knowledge, student-generated sources of evidence, prioritized criteria, and tradeoff considerations.
- Evaluate a solution to a complex real-world problem, based on scientific knowledge, student-generated sources of evidence, prioritized criteria, and tradeoff considerations.

COMMON CORE STATE STANDARDS FOR MATHEMATICS

MATHEMATICAL PRACTICES

- MP1. Make sense of problems and persevere in solving them.
- MP3. Construct viable arguments and critique the reasoning of others.
- MP5. Use appropriate tools strategically.
- MP6. Attend to precision.
- MP7. Look for and make use of structure.
- MP8. Look for and express regularity in repeated reasoning.

COMMON CORE STATE STANDARDS FOR ENGLISH LANGUAGE ARTS

READING STANDARDS

- RI.9–10.1. Cite strong and thorough textual evidence to support analysis of what the text says explicitly as well as inferences drawn from the text. a. Develop factual, interpretive, and evaluative questions for further exploration of the topic(s).
- RI.9–10.2. Determine a central idea of a text and analyze its development over the course of the text, including how it emerges and is shaped and refined by specific details; provide an objective summary of the text.
- RI.9–10.3. Analyze how the author unfolds an analysis or series of ideas or events, including the order in which the points are made, how they are introduced and developed, and the connections that are drawn between them.
- RI.9–10.4. Determine the meaning of words and phrases as they are used in a text, including figurative, connotative, and technical meanings; analyze the cumulative impact of specific word choices on meaning and tone (e.g., how the language of a court opinion differs from that of a newspaper).
- RI.9–10.6. Determine an author's point of view or purpose in a text and analyze how an author uses rhetoric to advance that point of view or purpose.
- RI.9–10.8. Delineate and evaluate the argument and specific claims in a text, assessing whether the reasoning is valid and the evidence is relevant and sufficient; identify false statements and fallacious reasoning.

- RI.9–10.10. By the end of grade 9, read and comprehend literary nonfiction in the grades 9–10 text complexity band proficiently, with scaffolding as needed at the high end of the range. Read and comprehend literary nonfiction at the high end of the grades 9–10 text complexity band independently and proficiently.
- RI.9–10.6. Determine an author's point of view or purpose in a text and analyze how an author uses rhetoric to advance that point of view or purpose.
- RI.9–10.8. Delineate and evaluate the argument and specific claims in a text, assessing whether the reasoning is valid and the evidence is relevant and sufficient; identify false statements and fallacious reasoning.
- RI.9–10.10. By the end of grade 9, read and comprehend literary nonfiction in the grades 9–10 text complexity band proficiently, with scaffolding as needed at the high end of the range. Read and comprehend literary nonfiction at the high end of the grades 9–10 text complexity band independently and proficiently.

WRITING STANDARDS

- W.9–10.1a-e Write arguments to support claims in an analysis of substantive topics or texts, using valid reasoning and relevant and sufficient evidence. Explore and inquire into areas of interest to formulate an argument.

    k) Introduce precise claim(s), distinguish the claim(s) from alternate or opposing claims, and create an organization that establishes clear relationships among claim(s), counterclaims, reasons, and evidence.
    l) Develop claim(s) and counterclaims fairly, supplying evidence for each while pointing out the strengths and limitations of both in a manner that anticipates the audience's knowledge level and concerns.
    m) Use words, phrases, and clauses to link the major sections of the text, create cohesion, and clarify the relationships between claim(s) and reasons, between reasons and evidence, and between claim(s) and counterclaims.
    n) Establish and maintain a formal style and objective tone while attending to the norms and conventions of the discipline in which they are writing.
    o) Provide a concluding statement or section that follows from and supports the argument presented.

- W.9–10.2a-f Write informative/explanatory texts to examine and convey complex ideas, concepts, and information clearly and accurately through the effective selection, organization, and analysis of content.

    a) Introduce a topic; organize complex ideas, concepts, and information to make important connections and distinctions; include formatting (e.g., headings), graphics (e.g., figures, tables), and multimedia when useful to aiding comprehension.
    b) Develop the topic with well-chosen, relevant, and sufficient facts, extended definitions, concrete details, quotations, or other information and examples appropriate to the audience's knowledge of the topic.
    c) Use appropriate and varied transitions to link the major sections of the text, create cohesion, and clarify the relationships among complex ideas and concepts.

Continued

Table 4.13 (*continued*)

> d) Use precise language and domain-specific vocabulary to manage the complexity of the topic.
> e) Establish and maintain a formal style and objective tone while attending to the norms and conventions of the discipline in which they are writing.
> f) Provide a concluding statement or section that follows from and supports the information or explanation presented (e.g., articulating implications or the significance of the topic).
>
> - W.9–10.4. Produce clear and coherent writing in which the development, organization, and style are appropriate to task, purpose, and audience.
> - W.9–10.5. Develop and strengthen writing as needed by planning, revising, editing, rewriting, or trying a new approach, focusing on addressing what is most significant for a specific purpose and audience.
> - W.9–10.7. Conduct short as well as more sustained research projects to answer a question (including a self-generated question) or solve a problem; narrow or broaden the inquiry when appropriate; synthesize multiple sources on the subject, demonstrating understanding of the subject under investigation.
> - W.9–10.8. Gather relevant information from multiple authoritative print and digital sources, using advanced searches effectively; assess the usefulness of each source in answering the research question; integrate information into the text selectively to maintain the flow of ideas, avoiding plagiarism and following a standard format for citation.
> - W.9–10.9a-b. Draw evidence from literary or informational texts to support analysis, reflection, and research.
>
> a) Apply *grades 9–10 Reading standards* to literature (e.g., "Analyze how an author draws on and transforms source material in a specific work.
> b) Apply *grades 9–10 Reading standards* to literary nonfiction (e.g., "Delineate and evaluate the argument and specific claims in a text, assessing whether the reasoning is valid and the evidence is relevant and sufficient; identify false statements and fallacious reasoning.
>
> - W.9–10.10 Write routinely over extended time frames (time for research, reflection, and revision) and shorter time frames (a single sitting or a day or two) for a range of tasks, purposes, and audiences.
>
> ### *SPEAKING AND LISTENING STANDARDS*
>
> - SL.9–10.1a-d. Engage effectively in a range of collaborative discussions (one-on-one, in groups, and teacher-led) with diverse partners on *grade 10 topics, texts, and issues,* building on others' ideas and expressing their own clearly.
>
> a) Come to discussions prepared, having read or studied required material; explicitly draw on that preparation by referring to evidence on the topic, text, or issue to probe and reflect on ideas under discussion.
> b) Follow rules for collegial discussions, set specific goals and deadlines, and define individual roles as needed.
> c) Pose and respond to specific questions with elaboration and detail by making comments that contribute to the topic, text, or issue under discussion.

> d) Review the key ideas expressed and demonstrate understanding of multiple perspectives through reflection and paraphrasing.
> e) Seek to understand and communicate with individuals from different perspectives and cultural backgrounds.
>
> - SL.9–10.2. Interpret information presented in diverse media and formats (e.g., visually, quantitatively, orally) and explain how it contributes to a topic, text, or issue under study.
> - SL.9–10.4. Present claims and findings, sequencing ideas logically and using pertinent descriptions, facts, and details to accentuate main ideas or themes; use appropriate eye contact, adequate volume, and clear pronunciation.
> - SL.9–10.6 Acquire and use accurately general academic and domain-specific words and phrases, sufficient for reading, writing, speaking, and listening at the college and career readiness level; demonstrate independence in gathering vocabulary knowledge when considering a word or phrase important to comprehension or expression.
>
> ## *LANGUAGE STANDARDS*
>
> - L.9–10.1a-b. Demonstrate command of the conventions of standard English grammar and usage when writing or speaking.
>
>   a) Use parallel structure.
>   b) Use various types of phrases (noun, verb, adjectival, adverbial, participial, prepositional, absolute) and clauses (independent, dependent; noun, relative, adverbial) to convey specific meanings and add variety and interest to writing or presentations.
>
> - L.9–10.2a-c. Demonstrate command of the conventions of standard English capitalization, punctuation, and spelling when writing.
>
>   a) Use a semicolon (and perhaps a conjunctive adverb) to link two or more closely related independent clauses.
>   b) Use a colon to introduce a list or quotation.
>   c) Spell correctly.
>
> - L.9–10.3a. Write and edit work so that it conforms to the guidelines in a style manual (e.g., *MLA Handbook*, Turabian's *Manual for Writers*) appropriate for the discipline and writing type.
>
> ## *FRAMEWORK FOR 21ST CENTURY LEARNING*
> Information Literacy; Media Literacy; ICT Literacy; Flexibility and Adaptability; Initiative and Self-Direction; Social and Cross Cultural Skills; Productivity and Accountability; Leadership and Responsibility

TEACHER BACKGROUND INFORMATION

- You should share with the students a calendar for accomplishing the various products that need to be done in order to meet the challenge. You may wish to organize this calendar of work by the EDP steps [Identify the problem, Brainstorm ideas and conduct background research, Create a plan (e.g., by sketching designs, formulating processes), Build (this may mean building an

object or formulating a process or solution), Test, Redesign, Share solutions], indicating when each phase of the EDP should be completed. Alternatively, you could organize the calendar of work by the deliverables

- Identify your innovation

- Create a diagram (drawn, computer-generated, etc.)

- Thoroughly describe how the innovation works

- Create a cost-benefit ratio of creating your innovative energy source

- Determine the approach to market the innovation to as many people as possible

- Determine a conservative amount of kilowatt-hours an individual unit produces per day

  - Use your knowledge of other energy sources (wind, hydro-electric, solar, etc.) to determine your amount

- Estimate the amount of fossil fuels that will not be used when your innovation is scaled up to the entire country or world

  - Your estimate must be supported by realistic data and the appropriate mathematics must be shown to justify your estimate.

COMMON MISCONCEPTIONS

Students will have various types of prior knowledge about the concepts introduced in this lesson. Table 4.14 outlines some common misconceptions students may have concerning these concepts. Because of the breadth of students' experiences, it is not possible to anticipate every misconception that students may bring as they approach this lesson. Incorrect or inaccurate prior understanding of concepts can influence student learning in the future, however, so it is important to be alert to misconceptions such as those presented in the table.

Table 4.14. Common Misconceptions About the Concepts in Lesson 4

Topic	Student Misconception	Explanation
Engineering Design Process (EDP)	Engineers use only the scientific process to solve problems in their work.	The scientific method is used to test predictions and explanations about the world. The EDP, on the other hand, is used to create a solution to a problem through testing and redesign. In reality, engineers use both processes (see Teacher Background section in Lesson 2 for more information about the differences and similarities between the scientific method and the EDP).

PREPARATION FOR LESSON 4

Review the Teacher Background Information provided (p. 70), and preview the videos and websites recommended in the Learning Plan Components section below.

LEARNING PLAN COMPONENTS

Introductory Activity/Engagement

Connection to the Challenge: Begin each day of this lesson by directing students' attention to the driving question for the module, asking "How can electricity be generated in a renewable/sustainable way for use in everyday life?" Remind students of the module challenge each day and hold a brief student discussion of how their learning in the previous days' lesson(s) contributed to their ability to create their innovation for the final challenge. You may wish to hold a class discussion, creating a class list of key ideas on chart paper or the board, or you may wish to have students create a STEM Research Notebook entry with this information.

Science Class and Mathematics, ELA and Social Studies Connections: Remind students of the module challenge. Have students refer to the Energy Innovation Challenge handouts from Lesson 1 (see pp. 61–62), telling students:

You and your fellow team members have decided to start a company that will change the way the world uses energy. Your primary goal is to create an innovative power source that is both sustainable and renewable. It can be something entirely new, a spinoff on a present technology, or a creative mixture of several technologies. In order to be a profitable company, the cost-benefit ratio of creating your innovative energy source must be considered as well as your ability to market the innovation to as many people as possible. Furthermore, your team must consider all the ways your innovation will impact the environment and the world's economy. In order to convince investors, politicians, and everyday people that your innovation is worthwhile, your team must accomplish the tasks outlined on the Energy Innovation Challenge handout.

Distribute the Energy Innovation Challenge rubric and Individual Contribution rubric attached at the end of this lesson (see pp. 113–116), and review the rubrics with the class.

Activity/Exploration

Science Class and Mathematics, ELA and Social Studies Connections: Review the steps of the EDP with students and ask how their teams might be able to use the EDP to address the Energy Innovation Challenge. Tell students that the Test step of the EDP will be their project presentations, and that they will reflect on what modifications they could make based on feedback from other students. Have each team create a plan for completing their work, using the EDP as a guide. Have student teams create their challenge solutions.

Explanation

Science Class and Mathematics, ELA and Social Studies Connections: Have each students team present its innovation to the class. Each student should evaluate the presentation using the Energy Innovation Challenge rubric and note suggestions and comments.

Elaboration/Application of Knowledge

Science Class and Mathematics, ELA and Social Studies Connections: Have each team review the rubrics their classmates completed for their project presentations. Have each student write a short paper on how they would revise their project based upon this feedback.

Evaluation/Assessment

Students may be assessed on the following performance tasks and other measures listed.

Performance Tasks

- Innovation Rubric

Other Measures

- Participation in class discussions

Energy Innovation Challenge Rubric

	Expert (4)	Competent (3)	Emerging (2)	Did not meet expectations (1)	Score
Innovation Comments	The innovation is a creative, **_new_** form of a renewable and sustainable energy source. It is grounded in science and has the potential to generate a large amount of energy for the world.	The innovation is a creative derivative of a present technology or idea. It is grounded in science and has the potential to generate a large amount of energy for the world.	The innovation is a derivative of a present technology or idea but is only slightly different than what already exist or has been imagined by others. It is grounded in science and has the potential to generate a large amount of energy for the world.	The innovation is too similar to a present day energy source or idea for an energy source.	
Design Comments	The design of the energy source is aesthetically pleasing and thorough in its design. It includes schematics of its inner-workings (For students who imagine an idea that does not use turbine/generators to create energy or forms similar to photovoltaic cells, the inner-workings of the energy source does not have to be created) as well as the outer portion of the energy source.	The design of the energy source is aesthetically pleasing and thorough in its design. The schematics of its inner-workings are not as thorough as the outer portion of the energy source.	The design of the energy source is decent and thorough in its design. It does not include schematics of its inner-workings but does include the outer portion of the energy source.	The design is drawn haphazardly and is difficult to understand. There are no schematics of the inner-workings of the energy source.	
Description Comments	Students go through great lengths to describe their innovation and how it works to the fullest extent possible. The description of how it works is based in scientific facts and theories.	Students do a decent job at describing their innovation and how it works. The description of how it works is based in scientific facts and theories.	Students do a thorough job describing what the innovation does but does not adequately describe how it works. The description is only loosely based in scientific facts and theories.	The student poorly describes the innovation and does not address how it works.	

Continued

Energy Innovation Challenge Rubric (*continued*)

	Expert (4)	Competent (3)	Emerging (2)	Did not meet expectations (1)	Score
Power Output Comments	Students base their proposed power output (in Watts) on present day energy sources and gives logical reasons for their estimates.	Students base their proposed power output (in Watts) on present day energy sources and give adequate reasons for their estimates.	Students base their proposed power output (in Watts) on present day energy sources but does give logical reasons for their estimates.	Students' give an outlandishly low or high power output that does not use present day technology to base their findings.	
World Energy Contribution Comments	Students give a feasible estimate for the number of their innovation that can be created in the future. In conjunction with this number and their estimate for its power output, students accurately calculate the amount of energy this number of their innovation will create, compare its future energy demands, and calculate the percentage of their innovations power production to the future world's consumption.	Students meet the criteria in the previous column but the number of units for their innovation is overestimated with regard to the space they need and the likely space available in the future.	Students meet the criteria in the first column minus one of the calculations.	Students meet the criteria in the first column minus two or more of the calculations.	
Total Score					

Individual Contribution to Energy Innovation Challenge Rubric

	Expert	Competent	Emerging	Did not meet expectations
Fact Checker and Editor	All of the data are checked and verified. The presentation is void of mistakes and all writing is grammatically perfect.	Most of the data are checked and verified. The presentation is mostly void of mistakes and all writing is grammatically perfect.	Much of the data are inaccurate. The presentation has mistakes and some of the writing has grammatical mistakes.	The factor checker did not do his/ her job according to the other team members.
Marketer	The marketer clearly considered the needs and motivations of all demographics and appealed to both sides respectfully and wisely. The presentation has creative ads for each demographic	The marketer considered the needs and motivations of all demographics and appealed to all sides respectfully and wisely. The ads in the presentation are lacking key motivators for one or two of the demographics.	The marketer considered the needs and motivations of all demographics and appealed to both sides but demonstrated bias (e.g., conveyed sarcasm or sanctimony) in one or more of the ads in the presentation.	The marketer did not consider the needs or motivations of one or more of the demographics.
Economist	The economist strongly considered the economic impact her team's innovation would have on the world economy, stating hypotheses for how a downturn in oil production would shift wealth and power as well as impact struggles for resources.	The economist considered the economic impact her team's innovation would have on the world economy, stating hypotheses for how a downturn in oil production would shift wealth.	The economist poorly considered the economic impact her team's innovation would have on the world economy. She did not consider how a downturn in oil production would shift wealth from one entity to the other or how that shift would alter power struggles.	The economist did not consider any economic impact beyond the wealth a few individuals would make on the innovation or the savings that would be passed along to the consumer.

Continued

Individual Contribution to Energy Innovation Challenge Rubric

	Expert	Competent	Emerging	Did not meet expectations
Environmentalist	The environmentalist strongly considered the ecological impact her team's innovation would have on the world. She addressed how it may affect the atmosphere, soil, and the amount of land it would use. Her portion of the presentation was clear, concise and easy to read.	The environmentalist considered the ecological impact her team's innovation would have on the world. She addressed how it may affect the atmosphere, soil, and the amount of land it would use. Her portion of the presentation was decently written.	The environmentalist decently considered the ecological impact her team's innovation would have on the world. She addressed only one of the criteria listed in the first column. Her portion of the presentation was poorly written.	The environmentalist worked from the assumption that her team's innovation would have no carbon footprint and thus no footprint at all. Little to no reporting on the innovation's impact on the environment was given.
Presenter	The presenter clearly studied each members' contribution to the project, conferred with them, practiced her presentation, and gave a clear, cogent, and coherent presentation.	The presenter studied each members' contribution to the project and conferred with them to ensure accuracy. Her presentation was decently clear, cogent, and coherent.	The presenter briefly reviewed the members' contribution but did not confer with them for accuracy. There are a few mistakes and the presentation was only slightly coherent.	The presenter did not review the other members' contribution and the presentation was poor.
Score				

REFERENCES

Peters-Burton, E. E., Seshaiyer, P., Burton, S. R., Drake-Patrick, J., & Johnson, C. C. 2015. The STEM road map for grades 9-12. In C. C. Johnson, E. E. Peters-Burton, & T. J. Moore (Eds.), *STEM road map: A framework for integrated STEM education* (pp. 124–162). New York, NY: Routledge.

TRANSFORMING LEARNING WITH REBUILDING THE NATURAL ENVIRONMENT AND THE *STEM ROAD MAP CURRICULUM SERIES*

Carla C. Johnson

This chapter serves as a conclusion to the Rebuilding the Natural Environment integrated STEM curriculum module, but it is just the beginning of the transformation of your classroom that is possible through use of the *STEM Road Map Curriculum Series*. In this book, many key resources have been provided to make learning meaningful for your students through integration of science, technology, engineering, and mathematics, as well as social studies and English language arts, into powerful problem- and project-based instruction. First, the Rebuilding the Natural Environment curriculum is grounded in the latest theory of learning for students in grade 1 specifically. Second, as your students work through this module, they engage in using the engineering design process (EDP) and build prototypes like engineers and STEM professionals in the real world. Third, students acquire important knowledge and skills grounded in national academic standards in mathematics, English language arts, science, and 21st century skills that will enable their learning to be deeper, retained longer, and applied throughout, illustrating the critical connections within and across disciplines. Finally, authentic formative assessments, including strategies for differentiation and addressing misconceptions, are embedded within the curriculum activities.

The Rebuilding the Natural Environment curriculum in the Optimizing the Human Condition STEM Road Map theme can be used in single-content classrooms (e.g., mathematics) where there is only one teacher or expanded to include multiple teachers and content areas across classrooms. Through the exploration of the Energy Innovation Challenge, students engage in a real-world STEM problem on the first

DOI: 10.4324/9781003261711-8

day of instruction and gather necessary knowledge and skills along the way in the context of solving the problem.

The other topics in the *STEM Road Map Curriculum Series* are designed in a similar manner, and NSTA Press and Routledge have published additional volumes in this series for this and other grade levels, and have plans to publish more.

For an up-to-date list of volumes in the series, please visit https://www.routledge.com/STEM-Road-Map-Curriculum-Series/book-series/SRM (for titles co-published by Routledge and NSTA Press), or https://www.nsta.org/book-series/stem-road-map-curriculum (for titles published by NSTA Press).

If you are interested in professional development opportunities focused on the STEM Road Map specifically or integrated STEM or STEM programs and schools overall, contact the lead editor of this project, Dr. Carla C. Johnson, Professor of Science Education at NC State University (carlacjohnson@ncsu.edu). Someone from the team will be in touch to design a program that will meet your individual, school, or district needs.

APPENDIX

CONTENT STANDARDS ADDRESSED
IN THIS MODULE

NEXT GENERATION SCIENCE STANDARDS

Table A1 (p. 120) lists the science and engineering practices, disciplinary core ideas, and crosscutting concepts this module addresses. The supported performance expectations are as follows:

- HS-PS3–3 Design, build, and refine a device that works within given constraints to convert one form of energy into another form of energy.

- HS-LS2–7 Design, evaluate, and refine a solution for reducing the impacts of human activities on the environment and biodiversity.

- HS-ETS1–3 Evaluate a solution to a complex real-world problem based on prioritized criteria and trade-offs that account for a range of constraints, including cost, safety, reliability, and aesthetics as well as possible social, cultural, and environmental impacts.

Table A1. Next Generation Science Standards (NGSS)

Science and Engineering Practices

CONSTRUCTING EXPLANATIONS AND DESIGNING SOLUTIONS

- Constructing explanations and designing solutions in 9–12 builds on K–8 experiences and progresses to explanations and designs that are supported by multiple and independent student-generated sources of evidence consistent with scientific ideas, principles, and theories.

- Design, evaluate, and/or refine a solution to a complex real-world problem, based on scientific knowledge, student-generated sources of evidence, prioritized criteria, and tradeoff considerations.

- Evaluate a solution to a complex real-world problem, based on scientific knowledge, student-generated sources of evidence, prioritized criteria, and tradeoff considerations.

Disciplinary Core Ideas

PS3.A. DEFINITIONS OF ENERGY

- At the macroscopic scale, energy manifests itself in multiple ways, such as in motion, sound, light, and thermal energy.

PS3.D. ENERGY IN CHEMICAL PROCESSES

- Although energy cannot be destroyed, it can be converted to less useful forms—for example, to thermal energy in the surrounding environment.

ETS1.A. DEFINING AND DELIMITING AN ENGINEERING PROBLEM

- Criteria and constraints also include satisfying any requirements set by society, such as taking issues of risk mitigation into account, and they should be quantified to the extent possible and stated in such a way that one can tell if a given design meets them.

LS2.C. ECOSYSTEM DYNAMICS, FUNCTIONING, AND RESILIENCE

- Anthropogenic changes (induced by human activity) in the environment—including habitat destruction, pollution, introduction of invasive species, overexploitation, and climate change—can disrupt an ecosystem and threaten the survival of some species.

LS4.D. BIODIVERSITY AND HUMANS

- Biodiversity is increased by the formation of new species (speciation) and decreased by the loss of species (extinction).

- Humans depend on the living world for the resources and other benefits provided by biodiversity. But human activity is also having adverse impacts on biodiversity through overpopulation, overexploitation, habitat destruction, pollution, introduction of invasive species, and climate change. Thus sustaining biodiversity so that ecosystem functioning and productivity are maintained is essential to supporting and enhancing life on Earth. Sustaining biodiversity also aids humanity by preserving landscapes of recreational or inspirational value.

ETS1.B. DEVELOPING POSSIBLE SOLUTIONS

- When evaluating solutions it is important to take into account a range of constraints including cost, safety, reliability and aesthetics and to consider social, cultural and environmental impacts.

Continued

Table A1. (*continued*)

Crosscutting Concepts

ENERGY AND MATTER

- Changes of energy and matter in a system can be described in terms of energy and matter flows into, out of, and within that system.

STABILITY AND CHANGE

- Much of science deals with constructing explanations of how things change and how they remain stable.

CONNECTIONS TO ENGINEERING, TECHNOLOGY, AND APPLICATIONS OF SCIENCE

- Influence of Science, Engineering and Technology on Society and the Natural World

- Modern civilization depends on major technological systems. Engineers continuously modify these technological systems by applying scientific knowledge and engineering design practices to increase benefits while decreasing costs and risks.

Source: NGSS Lead States. 2013. Next Generation Science Standards: For states, by states. Washington, DC: National Academies Press. *www.nextgenscience.org/next-generation-science-standards.*

Table A2. Common Core Mathematics and English Language Arts (ELA) Standards

MATHEMATICAL PRACTICES	READING STANDARDS
• MP1. Make sense of problems and persevere in solving them. • MP3. Construct viable arguments and critique the reasoning of others. • MP4. Model with mathematics. • MP5. Use appropriate tools strategically. • MP6. Attend to precision. • MP7. Look for and make use of structure. • MP8. Look for and express regularity in repeated reasoning.	• RI.9–10.1. Cite strong and thorough textual evidence to support analysis of what the text says explicitly as well as inferences drawn from the text.a. Develop factual, interpretive, and evaluative questions for further exploration of the topic(s). • RI.9–10.2. Determine a central idea of a text and analyze its development over the course of the text, including how it emerges and is shaped and refined by specific details; provide an objective summary of the text. • RI.9–10.3. Analyze how the author unfolds an analysis or series of ideas or events, including the order in which the points are made, how they are introduced and developed, and the connections that are drawn between them.
MATHEMATICAL CONTENT • BF.A.1.a. Determine an explicit expression, a recursive process, or steps for calculation from a context. • CED.A.1. Create equations and inequalities in one variable and use them to solve problems. • CED.A.2. Create equations in two or more variables to represent relationships between quantities; graph equations on coordinate axes with labels and scales. • REI.C.5. Prove that, given a system of two equations in two variables, replacing one equation by the sum of that equation and a multiple of the other produces a system with the same solutions. • REI.C.6. Solve systems of linear equations exactly and approximately (e.g., with graphs), focusing on pairs of linear equations in two variables. • REI.C.10. Understand that the graph of an equation in two variables is the set of all its solutions plotted in the coordinate plane, often forming a curve (which could be a line). • REI.C.11. Explain why the x-coordinates of the points where the graphs of the equations $y = f(x)$ and $y = g(x)$ intersect are the solutions of the equation $f(x) = g(x)$; find the solutions approximately, e.g., using technology to graph the functions, make tables of values, or find successive approximations	• RI.9–10.4. Determine the meaning of words and phrases as they are used in a text, including figurative, connotative, and technical meanings; analyze the cumulative impact of specific word choices on meaning and tone (e.g., how the language of a court opinion differs from that of a newspaper). • RI.9–10.6. Determine an author's point of view or purpose in a text and analyze how an author uses rhetoric to advance that point of view or purpose. • RI.9–10.8. Delineate and evaluate the argument and specific claims in a text, assessing whether the reasoning is valid and the evidence is relevant and sufficient; identify false statements and fallacious reasoning. • RI.9–10.10. By the end of grade 9, read and comprehend literary nonfiction in the grades 9–10 text complexity band proficiently, with scaffolding as needed at the high end of the range. Read and comprehend literary nonfiction at the high end of the grades 9–10 text complexity band independently and proficiently. • RI.9–10.6. Determine an author's point of view or purpose in a text and analyze how an author uses rhetoric to advance that point of view or purpose. • RI.9–10.8. Delineate and evaluate the argument and specific claims in a text, assessing whether the reasoning is valid and the evidence is relevant and sufficient; identify false statements and fallacious reasoning.

Continued

Table A2. (*continued*)

• REI.C.12. Graph the solutions to a linear inequality in two variables as a half-plane (excluding the boundary in the case of a strict inequality), and graph the solution set to a system of linear inequalities in two variables as the intersection of the corresponding half-planes.

• IF.B.4. For a function that models a relationship between two quantities, interpret key features of graphs and tables in terms of the quantities, and sketch graphs showing key features given a verbal description of the relationship. Key features include: intercepts; intervals where the function is increasing, decreasing, positive, or negative; relative maximums and minimums; symmetries; end behavior; and periodicity

• IF.B.5. Relate the domain of a function to its graph and, where applicable, to the quantitative relationship it describes. For example, if the function h(n) gives the number of person-hours it takes to assemble n engines in a factory, then the positive integers would be an appropriate domain for the function.

• IF.B.6. Calculate and interpret the average rate of change of a function (presented symbolically or as a table) over a specified interval. Estimate the rate of change from a graph.

• RI.9–10.10. By the end of grade 9, read and comprehend literary nonfiction in the grades 9–10 text complexity band proficiently, with scaffolding as needed at the high end of the range. Read and comprehend literary nonfiction at the high end of the grades 9–10 text complexity band independently and proficiently.

WRITING STANDARDS

• W.9–10.1a-e. Write arguments to support claims in an analysis of substantive topics or texts, using valid reasoning and relevant and sufficient evidence. Explore and inquire into areas of interest to formulate an argument.

a) Introduce precise claim(s), distinguish the claim(s) from alternate or opposing claims, and create an organization that establishes clear relationships among claim(s), counterclaims, reasons, and evidence.

b) Develop claim(s) and counterclaims fairly, supplying evidence for each while pointing out the strengths and limitations of both in a manner that anticipates the audience's knowledge level and concerns.

c) Use words, phrases, and clauses to link the major sections of the text, create cohesion, and clarify the relationships between claim(s) and reasons, between reasons and evidence, and between claim(s) and counterclaims.

d) Establish and maintain a formal style and objective tone while attending to the norms and conventions of the discipline in which they are writing.

e) Provide a concluding statement or section that follows from and supports the argument presented.

• W.9–10.2a-f. Write informative/explanatory texts to examine and convey complex ideas, concepts, and information clearly and accurately through the effective selection, organization, and analysis of content.

a) Introduce a topic; organize complex ideas, concepts, and information to make important connections and distinctions; include formatting (e.g., headings), graphics (e.g., figures, tables), and multimedia when useful to aiding comprehension.

b) Develop the topic with well-chosen, relevant, and sufficient facts, extended definitions, concrete details, quotations, or other information and examples appropriate to the audience's knowledge of the topic.

Continued

Table A2. (*continued*)

	c) Use appropriate and varied transitions to link the major sections of the text, create cohesion, and clarify the relationships among complex ideas and concepts. d) Use precise language and domain-specific vocabulary to manage the complexity of the topic. e) Establish and maintain a formal style and objective tone while attending to the norms and conventions of the discipline in which they are writing. f) Provide a concluding statement or section that follows from and supports the information or explanation presented (e.g., articulating implications or the significance of the topic). • W.9–10.4 Produce clear and coherent writing in which the development, organization, and style are appropriate to task, purpose, and audience. • W.9–10.5. Develop and strengthen writing as needed by planning, revising, editing, rewriting, or trying a new approach, focusing on addressing what is most significant for a specific purpose and audience. • W.9–10.7. Conduct short as well as more sustained research projects to answer a question (including a self-generated question) or solve a problem; narrow or broaden the inquiry when appropriate; synthesize multiple sources on the subject, demonstrating understanding of the subject under investigation. • W.9–10.8. Gather relevant information from multiple authoritative print and digital sources, using advanced searches effectively; assess the usefulness of each source in answering the research question; integrate information into the text selectively to maintain the flow of ideas, avoiding plagiarism and following a standard format for citation. • W.9–10.9a-b. Draw evidence from literary or informational texts to support analysis, reflection, and research. a) Apply *grades 9–10 Reading standards* to literature (e.g., "Analyze how an author draws on and transforms source material in a specific work b) Apply *grades 9–10 Reading standards* to literary nonfiction (e.g., "Delineate and evaluate the argument and specific claims in a text, assessing whether the reasoning is valid and the evidence is relevant and sufficient; identify false statements and fallacious reasoning").

Continued

Table A2. (*continued*)

	• W.9–10.10 Write routinely over extended time frames (time for research, reflection, and revision) and shorter time frames (a single sitting or a day or two) for a range of tasks, purposes, and audiences.
	
	SPEAKING AND LISTENING STANDARDS
	• SL.9–10.1a-d. Engage effectively in a range of collaborative discussions (one-on-one, in groups, and teacher-led) with diverse partners on *grade 10 topics, texts, and issues*, building on others' ideas and expressing their own clearly.
	
	   a) Come to discussions prepared, having read or studied required material; explicitly draw on that preparation by referring to evidence on the topic, text, or issue to probe and reflect on ideas under discussion.
	   b) Follow rules for collegial discussions, set specific goals and deadlines, and define individual roles as needed.
	   c) Pose and respond to specific questions with elaboration and detail by making comments that contribute to the topic, text, or issue under discussion.
	   d) Review the key ideas expressed and demonstrate understanding of multiple perspectives through reflection and paraphrasing.
	   e) Seek to understand and communicate with individuals from different perspectives and cultural backgrounds.
	• SL.9–10.2. Interpret information presented in diverse media and formats (e.g., visually, quantitatively, orally) and explain how it contributes to a topic, text, or issue under study.
	
	• SL.9–10.4. Present claims and findings, sequencing ideas logically and using pertinent descriptions, facts, and details to accentuate main ideas or themes; use appropriate eye contact, adequate volume, and clear pronunciation.
	
	LANGUAGE STANDARDS
	• L.9–10.1a-b. Demonstrate command of the conventions of standard English grammar and usage when writing or speaking.
	
	   a) Use parallel structure.
	   b) Use various types of phrases (noun, verb, adjectival, adverbial, participial, prepositional, absolute) and clauses (independent, dependent; noun, relative, adverbial) to convey specific meanings and add variety and interest to writing or presentations.

Continued

Table A2. (*continued*)

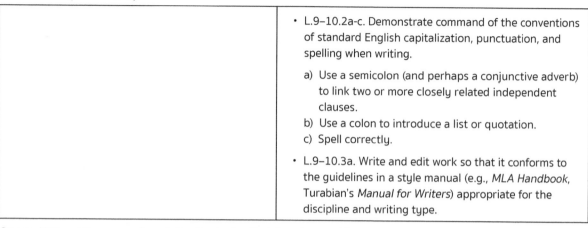

	• L.9–10.2a-c. Demonstrate command of the conventions of standard English capitalization, punctuation, and spelling when writing. a) Use a semicolon (and perhaps a conjunctive adverb) to link two or more closely related independent clauses. b) Use a colon to introduce a list or quotation. c) Spell correctly. • L.9–10.3a. Write and edit work so that it conforms to the guidelines in a style manual (e.g., *MLA Handbook*, Turabian's *Manual for Writers*) appropriate for the discipline and writing type.

Source: National Governors Association Center for Best Practices and Council of Chief State School Officers (NGAC and CCSSO). 2010. Common core state standards. Washington, DC: NGAC and CCSSO.

Table A3. 21st Century Skills from the Framework for 21st Century Learning

21st Century Skills	Learning Skills and Technology Tools	Teaching Strategies	Evidence of Success
INTERDISCIPLINARY THEMES • Global Awareness • Financial, Economic, Business and Entrepreneurial Literacy • Civic Literacy • Environmental Literacy	• Using 21st century skills to understand and address global issues. • Knowing how to make appropriate economic choices. • Understanding the role of the economy in society. • Using entrepreneurial skills to address complex issues. • Demonstrate knowledge and understanding of the environment and the circumstances and conditions affecting it. • Demonstrate knowledge and understanding of society's impact on the natural world. • Investigate and analyze environmental issues, and make accurate conclusions about effective solutions.	• Guide conversations on how energy production and consumption have shaped humankind economically, socially, and ecologically. • Provide students with resources to conduct independent research about the effect of oil dependency on the global economy, the environment, and world affairs. • Provide students with examples of entrepreneurial approaches to alternative energy sources and analyze these approaches in terms of economic and environmental impacts.	• Students gain and demonstrate an understanding of the positive and negative implications of using fossil fuels and of using renewable/ sustainable energy sources to meet society's demands for energy. • Students present their ideas for renewable/ sustainable energy sources that consider the energy needs of the present and future world population and consider the impact the sources may have in terms of the global economy and the environment.
LEARNING AND INNOVATION SKILLS • Creativity and Innovation • Critical Thinking and Problem Solving • Communication and Collaboration	• Use a wide range of idea creation techniques (such as brainstorming) to create new ideas and refine and evaluate those ideas. • Be open and responsive to new and diverse perspectives; incorporate group input and feedback into the work. • Demonstrate originality and inventiveness in work and understand the real world limits to adopting new ideas.	• Facilitate class discussion and student research about renewable/ sustainable energy sources, how they can be used to generate electricity, and the impact they have on the environment and the economy.	• Students independently and collaboratively synthesize information they gather on renewable/ sustainable energy sources. • Students individually present their findings about an energy source to their classmates.

Continued

Table A3. (*continued*)

21st Century Skills	Learning Skills and Technology Tools	Teaching Strategies	Evidence of Success
	• Analyze how parts of a whole interact with each other to produce overall outcomes in complex systems. • Effectively analyze and evaluate evidence, arguments, claims and beliefs and draw conclusions. • Solve various problems in both conventional and innovative ways. • Articulate thoughts and ideas effectively using oral, written and nonverbal communication skills in a variety of forms and contexts. • Listen effectively to decipher meaning, including knowledge, values, attitudes and intentions. • Use communication for a range of purposes (e.g. to inform, instruct, motivate and persuade). • Demonstrate ability to work effectively and respectfully with diverse teams. • Exercise flexibility and willingness to be helpful in making necessary compromises to accomplish a common goal. • Assume shared responsibility for collaborative work, and value the individual contributions made by each team member.		• Students work in teams to devise a plan for an innovative alternative energy source and present their innovative energy source to classmates.

Continued

NATIONAL SCIENCE TEACHING ASSOCIATION

Table A3. (*continued*)

INFORMATION, MEDIA AND TECHNOLOGY SKILLS • Information Literacy • Media Literacy • ICT Literacy	• Access information efficiently (time) and effectively (sources). • Evaluate information critically and competently. • Use information accurately and creatively for the issue or problem at hand. • Understand both how and why media messages are constructed, and for what purposes. • Use technology as a tool to research, organize, evaluate and communicate information.	• Require the use and examination of various reliable resources for information about renewable/sustainable energy.	• Students critically analyze and synthesize multiple streams of information about energy sources and develop reasonable conclusions to support their proposal of an innovative energy source. • Students will use reliable resources and cite these resources appropriately in their final product.
LIFE AND CAREER SKILLS • Flexibility and Adaptability • Initiative and Self-Direction • Social and Cross Cultural Skills • Productivity and Accountability • Leadership and Responsibility	• Adapt to varied roles, jobs responsibilities, schedules and contexts. • Incorporate feedback effectively. • Deal positively with praise, setbacks and criticism. • Understand, negotiate and balance diverse views and beliefs to reach workable solutions, particularly in multi-cultural environments. • Balance tactical (short-term) and strategic (long-term) goals. • Utilize time and manage workload efficiently. • Monitor, define, prioritize and complete tasks without direct oversight. • Reflect critically on past experiences in order to inform future progress. • Know when it is appropriate to listen and when to speak.	• Provide checkpoints for students to self-monitor their progress. • Create situations where students are able to work in groups collaboratively.	• Students will articulate their goals for each check point for the project and devise strategic plans to show progress toward their goals. • Students work effectively in collaborative groups and are clear about the role of each member. • Students take responsibility for their own learning.

Continued

Table A3. (*continued*)

21st Century Skills	Learning Skills and Technology Tools	Teaching Strategies	Evidence of Success
	• Conduct themselves in a respectable, professional manner. • Use interpersonal and problem-solving skills to influence and guide others toward a goal. • Leverage strengths of others to accomplish a common goal.		

Table A4. English Language Development Standards

ELD STANDARD 1: SOCIAL AND INSTRUCTIONAL LANGUAGE
English language learners communicate for Social and Instructional purposes within the school setting.
ELD STANDARD 2: THE LANGUAGE OF LANGUAGE ARTS
English language learners communicate information, ideas and concepts necessary for academic success in the content area of Language Arts.
ELD STANDARD 3: THE LANGUAGE OF MATHEMATICS
English language learners communicate information, ideas and concepts necessary for academic success in the content area of Mathematics
ELD STANDARD 4: THE LANGUAGE OF SCIENCE.
English language learners communicate information, ideas and concepts necessary for academic success in the content area of Science
ELD STANDARD 5: THE LANGUAGE OF SOCIAL STUDIES
English language learners communicate information, ideas and concepts necessary for academic success in the content area of Social Studies.

Source: WIDA, 2012, 2012 Amplification of the English language development standards: Kindergarten–grade 12, www.wida.us/standards/eld.aspx.

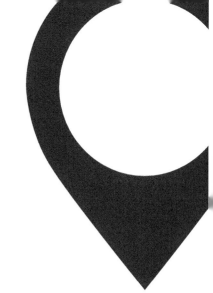

INDEX

Note: Page numbers in **bold type** refer to tables

For Product Safety Concerns and Information please contact our
EU representative GPSR@taylorandfrancis.com Taylor & Francis ASSOCIATION
Verlag GmbH, Kaufingerstraße 24, 80331 München, Germany